HYDROPONICS

HYDROPONICS
Growing without Soil

DUDLEY HARRIS
MSc

Easy-to-follow Instructions for the
Flatdweller, Modern Gardener and
Commercial Grower

THIS EDITION REVISED FOR
TEMPERATE ZONES BY

A. M. M. BERRIE
BSc PhD
AND IAN G. WALLS
NDH CDH A Inst PRA

DAVID & CHARLES
NEWTON ABBOT LONDON VANCOUVER

0 7153 6397 2
© Dudley Harris, 1966, 1974
Reprinted 1978

First Published by Purnell and Sons (S.A.) (Pty) Ltd, 1966
Third edition 1971
Completely revised edition published by David & Charles
(Publishers) Limited 1974

Printed in Great Britain by A. Wheaton & Co Ltd, Exeter
for David & Charles (Publishers) Limited
Brunel House, Newton Abbot, Devon

Contents

List of illustrations

IN TEXT

8

Preface to this edition

Why bother with chemicals, tanks and such things when all you have to do is to put seed in the ground, water it, and leave the rest to Nature. In short, what is hydroponics all about?

If you happen to live in a flat or house with or without a garden and wish to start a hobby that is fascinating; if you are a commercial grower of carnations, gladioli, chrysanthemums or want to become one; if you have no arable soil . . . then hydroponics should interest you.

Since its commercial beginnings in the 1930s many books have been written on the subject. Some are rather technical in their approach, while others lack sufficient practical details.

This book is intended to cover a very wide field of interest, being, in a way, both a practical instructional manual in small-scale hydroponics and a source of technical detail for the prospective commercial grower.

As a practical guide for the reader, certain products used by the authors have been mentioned by their trade names. It should be borne in mind, however, that other suitable alternatives are also available.

Many photographs have been used in order to illustrate more clearly the various stages in preparing hydroponics seed-trays or building concrete tanks.

It is sincerely hoped that this book will enable *anyone* to make a start with hydroponics.

While the main emphasis is on gravel culture, full details are also given on the use of sand, vermiculite, lignite and other materials such as peat as media.

To satisfy the more inquiring minds – and others with scientific backgrounds – elementary chemical arithmetic and formulae are presented in Chapter Nine.

There is also material of interest to the gardener in soil, particularly in Chapters Six, Ten, Eleven, Twelve and Thirteen.

In order to cater for this broad field the subject-matter has been divided into three parts:

PART I   will be of special interest to all prospective hydroponic growers with little or no previous knowledge of the subject;

PART II   will be of special interest both to the commercial grower and to the more technically-minded;

PART III   will be of interest to all gardeners, both soilless and in soil.

It is hoped that all the subject-matter will be found to be equally digestible.

D.A.H.
A.M.M.B.
I.G.W.

PART ONE

CHAPTER ONE

What is a plant?
How does it grow?

Before considering how to grow plants without soil, it is necessary to understand, as far as possible, how they grow in soil. In order to do this, however, a basic knowledge of what constitutes a plant is the first requirement.

It is visibly obvious that the higher plant body has three main parts while vegetative, and when it is reproductive a fourth structure arises. These are:

(1) roots,
(2) stems,
(3) leaves,
(4) flowers.

Like all complex organisms, plants are composed of microscopic units called cells, and the various parts of the plant are built up of these units. There are simple plants which consist of single cells, but these do not concern us unless they grow on the surface of our hydroponic bed.

Plant cells (Fig 1) differ from animal cells by being surrounded with a rigid wall or 'box' which is quite permeable to water and salts. This wall is composed of cellulose and is not living. Within this 'box', which is essentially the same as cardboard, there lies the living part of the cell. The names given to the whole of this living part is the protoplast, which is bounded by a membrane and contains a jelly-like substance, protoplasm. Here all the vital processes of the plant take place. The protoplasm must function

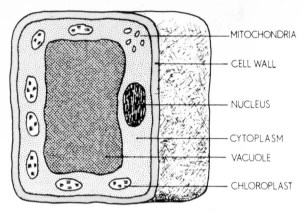

MITOCHONDRIA

CELL WALL

NUCLEUS

CYTOPLASM

VACUOLE

CHLOROPLAST

Fig 1 *Diagram of a living plant cell. The cell is bounded by a cellular wall which is inert with regard to the movement of water and salts into the vacuole. In the cytoplasm, which has a granular appearance, there is always a large nucleus, some mitochondria (see top right-hand corner) and, if green, many chloroplasts*

normally for the cell to live and prosper. A crude chemical analysis of the protoplasm shows that it is made up of proteins, nucleic acids, fatty substances, carbohydrates and minerals, but the bulk of the protoplasm is water. Plant cells also contain within the protoplasm many vacuoles. These appear as holes when viewed with a microscope, though the vacuole is not empty but contains a solution of salts and soluble organic substances. This type of vacuole is characteristic of plant cells and is much involved in the movement of water and salts, both in and out of the cell, and from one cell to another.

When living plant cells are examined in detail under a microscope the protoplasm is seen to be composed of a ground substance in which small objects are immersed. These small structures are collectively called cell organelles. The most prominent is the *nucleus*, which is concerned with the maintenance of production of proteins, and is also the structure that carries the genetic information. Plant cells have plastids, and those that are involved in the production of sugar from light are coloured green and called chloroplasts. In other cell types the plastids give rise to starch grains or contain pigment, as in the case of the cells in the

12

fruit of the tomato plant. Other small organelles need not concern us.

Let us return to the plant organs.

1. THE ROOT SYSTEM

Because the roots are underground the reader will be least familiar with them, but they are absolutely essential to the plant's well-being.

Roots serve the purpose of anchoring the plant in its growing medium (soil), as well as the vital role of absorbing water and the inorganic nutrients present in the soil.

Roots branch profusely, giving rise to a complex pattern. By means of repeated branching, a system of main roots and laterals is built up, and each root is clothed with fine hairs most clearly seen just behind the tip. The fine root hairs in this sub-terminal region absorb water and minerals. They do not last very long and are absent from the older parts of the root. It is those most recently formed that are the most active. The protoplasm is semi-permeable and has selective properties over the molecules which come in contact with it, allowing the accumulation of certain minerals in the vacuoles while preventing an excess build-up of others. The root hairs absorb water by a process called osmosis, and this is so important in understanding a plant's relationship to the soil that an attempt will be made to explain it as simply as possible.

Imagine a glass of water with one teaspoonful of sugar in it. If a small thimble made of parchment (which is permeable to water but not sugar) half filled with a sugar solution twice as strong as that in the glass is floated on the solution in the glass, it will be found that water will move into the thimble from the solution in the glass. This is because nature strives towards equilibrium and in the system just described this is achieved when the concentration inside the thimble and outside in the glass is the same. A more telling demonstration of the phenomenon of osmosis can be made if we substitute for the parchment thimble one made from the inside of a potato. In this case we use the protoplasm of the cells as our semi-permeable membrane.

13

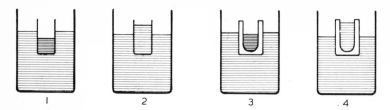

Fig 2 The uptake of water by osmosis in a parchment thimble (1 and 2) and in a potato thimble (3 and 4). In 1 and 3 a strong sugar solution is put in the thimbles, and after a while (2 and 4) water enters from the bathing solution

If the idea of the glass with the dilute sugar solution is considered as being the dilute soil solution or the nutrient and soil solution, and the solution in the thimble is thought of as corresponding with that in the cell vacuole of the plant, one can understand the manner in which a plant can absorb the water from the soil, or from a hydroponic solution, through its root hair cells (Fig 2).

Soil solutions might, in certain instances, become more concentrated than the solution in the vacuole of the root, with the result that the water could move out of the plant. While this circumstance is infrequent in all but alkaline soils and those flooded by salt water, it can be a frequent occurrence in solution culture or where fertilisers are used in large amounts. If water is removed from the cells by a concentrated solution, the cells undergo plasmolysis. The protoplast shrinks away from the cell wall and the cell does not possess much rigidity. As a result the organ collapses, and in the stem and leaves this is seen as wilting. Wilting, of course, also occurs when soils dry out to such an extent that there is no longer water available.

A cell fully gorged with water is said to be *turgid,* while one in which water has been removed to the point of plasmolysis is spoken of as *flaccid.* The analogy between a blown-up balloon and one which is not can be made, and in the case of herbaceous or 'soft' plants the maintenance of an upright stem depends on the cells being 'blown-up' or turgid.

2. SOIL

To understand hydroponics it is necessary to know something about the soil in which plants grow. Soil is a very complex material but may be conveniently divided into (a) an organic part and (b) an inorganic fraction.

The organic part of the soil is itself made up of two components – a larger non-living portion representing the plant and animal remains which are added to all soils, and a living portion consisting of bacteria, fungi, protozoa, small animals, worms and even mice. As a result of the activities of the living, the organic debris in the soil is eventually converted to *humus* which is distributed throughout the soil. Humus confers a blackness to soils and has much effect on its texture and water-holding capacity. Humus can also bind materials and in the early stages of its formation is a source of the plant nutrient nitrogen.

The 'non-living' or inorganic part of the soil consists of broken down rock particles either formed *in situ* or transported by wind, water or ice and can be classified according to size and chemical composition. After removing the large stones we find that the soil particles are either siliceous and are called sands and fine sands, depending on size, or are complex hydrated aluminium silicates making up the clays and, to a lesser extent, the larger silts. The nature of the rocks from which the soil is derived determines its composition. In addition to the particulate minerals of the soil there are some which are in solution in the water present in most soils. This weak mixture is called the *soil solution,* and the plant depends on this for its supplies of water and essential nutrients.

A soil, therefore, is a mixture of decomposed organic remains and chemically altered rock materials ranging in size from clays (particles less than 0·002 mm in diameter) through silt, fine sand, sand and gravel (particles larger than 2 mm diameter). Also present are water and gases (the soil air). The approximate percentages by volume of a few soil types are given in Table 1.

Like atmospheric air, soil air contains life-giving oxygen, but at a lower level than the atmosphere. Soil air also contains appreciably more carbon dioxide than the atmosphere. The oxygen is

TABLE 1

	Sandy Soil	Clay Soil
Mineral Matter	67%	53%
Made up of:		
Sand	85 pts	25 pts
Silt	10 pts	30 pts
Clay	5 pts	45 pts
Organic Matter %	3	5
Soil Air* %	21	11
Soil Water* %	7	30

*Measured at Field capacity. A dry soil would have increased amounts of air, while a wetter soil would have a higher water content.

NB. Percentage totals are approximate.

necessary for the respiration of the plant roots and the aerobic soil organisms, and if for any reason the level of oxygen is much reduced, neither the plants nor the very important bacteria and fungi which require that gas will prosper. For example, the formation of root hairs depends on the continued supply of oxygen to the root. Perhaps the most common cause of deprivation of oxygen in a soil is flooding.

Reverting to the root system, it has been seen that each rootlet is covered with thousands of root hairs capable of absorbing water and certain nutrient elements from the soil. Imagine the enormous area that all the root hairs on all the rootlets will cover when in contact with the millions of moist soil particles making up a soil (Fig 3). Each little hair will be responsible for absorbing its own quota of water and nutrient elements, which will rise through the stem to the leaves of the plant.

3. THE STEM

While not so elaborate in its ramification of the environment, the stem is as specialised as the root. Its function and form differ.

It is obvious to the most casual observer that the stem connects the roots to the leaves and that it conducts the water and

16

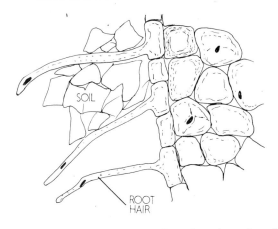

Fig 3 Root hairs absorbing water and nutrients from the soil spaces

minerals absorbed by the roots to the leaves. It also transports materials manufactured by the leaves to the roots. The stem then is concerned with the long-distance transport of materials in the plant, and its structure bears this out, being essentially a system of conduits in which fluids move vertically upwards and downwards.

4.   THE LEAVES

The leaf is the principal manufacturing organ of the plant. Here the process of photosynthesis takes place.

In the presence of sunlight and water the leaf can 'fix' the carbon dioxide of the atmosphere (present at a concentration of 300 ppm) to manufacture sugar. The remarkable green substance responsible for carrying out the chemical reactions that occur in the fixation of carbon dioxide is known as *chlorophyll*. The simple sugars produced in photosynthesis are utilised by the plant to provide energy and starting materials for the production of complex carbohydrates, fats, proteins, and other essential compounds.

The second important role of the leaf is that of air conditioning. By means of numerous little pores called *stomata,* mainly on the underside of the leaf, gases are exchanged between the

17

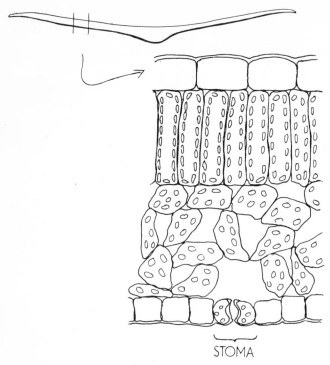

STOMA

Fig 4 Leaf section showing how the gases are exchanged between the inter-cellular spaces of the leaf and the atmosphere

intercellular spaces of the leaf and the atmosphere (see Fig 4). The main gases are oxygen and carbon dioxide (both implicated in photosynthesis and respiration), and water vapour (involved in air conditioning). The cells of the leaf lose water by evaporation and the water vapour which results is lost to the atmosphere through the stomata. The loss of water vapour is called *transpiration* and the evaporative process keeps the leaf cool when sunlight falls on it. On a sunny day, if there were no transpiration, the temperature of the leaf within 1 min would be so high that the leaf would not be able to carry out photosynthesis and other vital processes. Indeed, within a very short time the leaf would be 'cooked'.

However, the loss of water cannot proceed faster than the

supply to the leaf. If it does, the stomata will close and eventually the plant will wilt. It is important to realise that when a plant exhibits these symptoms, movement of carbon dioxide is restricted and the rate of photosynthesis will be reduced. Wilting should at all times be avoided. Often the plant shows wilt symptoms for a short while, recovering when water becomes available. This is called temporary wilting, but if the water stress is prolonged and the plant does not recover when water is freely available, it has reached the stage of permanent wilting and will die.

Respiration refers to the consumption of sugar in a process analagous to burning, the energy which is released being used in vital processes. It involves the uptake of oxygen and the liberation of carbon dioxide and water vapour, in fact the opposite to photosynthesis, where carbon dioxide and water are used to produce sugar and oxygen. All living tissues respire continuously, and it is vital that they do.

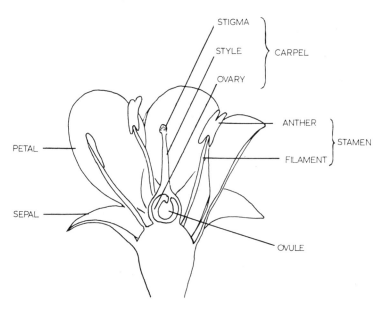

Fig 5 Section of the typical flower

19

5. THE FLOWER

The essential parts of the flower are the *stamens,* often considered equivalent to male parts, and the *carpels,* considered to correspond to female parts. The equating of these parts with structures found in male and female animals is not strictly correct, but it will suffice for us to consider the floral parts this way. Fig 5 shows the typical flower in section and we see that the stamen has two distinct parts, the stalk or *filament,* and the *anther* or pollen-bearing region. The *carpel* has a basal *ovary,* and a receptive structure, the *stigma,* at the end of an elongated *style.*

The first event in sexual reproduction is the transfer of pollen from the anther to the stigma. This constitutes *pollination* and can be brought about by insects, wind, or very occasionally water. On landing on the stigmatic surface a viable pollen grain will germinate to produce a *pollen-tube,* which penetrates the surface and grows down the style, eventually reaching an *ovule* in the ovary. *Fertilisation* occurs when there is fusion between a nucleus transferred from the pollen tube and a specialised nucleus, the *ovum,* of the ovule. Once this has taken place, a seed can start to develop within the ovary which becomes transformed into the fruit.

Most plants have stamens and carpels in the same flower, eg tomatoes, but some have flowers which have only stamens *or* carpels. Sometimes these 'unisexual' flowers are on the same plant, as in cucumber, but there are cases where plants have either all-staminal flowers or all carpellary. This last situation we find in asparagus.

Reproduction may take place asexually. This is familiar enough in plants which produce runners, offsets, bulbs, tubers, corms, etc. The taking of cuttings is a method of asexual reproduction.

6. MINERAL ELEMENTS

Though still concerned with the plant growing in soil, we now come to what is essentially common ground between soil and soil-less growing, namely the mineral elements of nutrient status.

These are elements absorbed by the plant from the soil solution in which they are dissolved. Normal growth and development are impossible without them.

There are six *macro* (major) and six *micro* (minor) or *trace* elements that are obtained from the soil solution. The distinction is drawn between these two classes of nutrients on the basis of the amounts required by the plant for healthy growth. The terms major and minor were once commonly used, but it is much better not to use them now, as they imply quite wrongly that the former group is important and the latter is not. It should be emphasised that the trace elements are every bit as important to the well-being of the plant as the macro elements.

The macro elements include nitrogen, phosphorus, potassium, calcium, magnesium and sulphur. Among the known essential elements required in small amounts are iron, boron, manganese, copper, zinc and molybdenum. Iron is unique in that the amount the plant requires is somewhat greater than that of the other elements in this list – indeed it occupies a place between the macro and trace elements.

Recently sodium and chlorine have been shown to be necessary for plant growth, but if you live within 1,000 miles of the sea, enough of these two elements is washed down by rain to satisfy the plant's needs.

Large amounts of carbon, hydrogen and oxygen are present in the plant's body, and these are rightly considered as macro nutrients. They are not obtained from minerals but from the gases of the atmosphere and water.

Smaller amounts of exotic elements such as vanadium and gold are found in plants, and most plants have fairly large quantities of aluminium in their bodies. Some, notably the grasses, accumulate silica in certain cells. There is no known metabolic role for the elements just mentioned, but excess amounts of aluminium are harmful to the plant.

The role each mineral plays in plant metabolism is more or less known, although in some cases their exact function is obscure, eg boron. Plant physiologists have been experimenting, over the last 100 years, to fill the gaps in our knowledge of mineral element function.

The following is a summary of the role of the mineral elements in plant metabolism.

Nitrogen. This is found as an integral part of the molecules of proteins, nucleic acids, chlorophyll and other less common but vital substances. Excess amounts of this element result in dark green lush growth (soft), while deficiency gives rise to small yellow-green plants sometimes showing red coloration. Branching is much reduced.

Phosphorus. This element is present in nucleic acids and is also involved in transferring chemical energy. Seeds and fruits are always rich in this element. Phosphorus-deficient plants are dwarfed, blue-green, and have reddish coloration.

Potassium. Potassium is not found as an integral part of an organic molecule, but is concerned with the regulation of the salt and water balance of the cell. Growing points are always rich in this element. Deficiency produces leaf scorch, especially along the leaf margin, and in less severe cases the cells of the leaf and the stomata are smaller and fewer. The symptoms of deficiency are not always apparent and diagnosis can be difficult.

Calcium. The main function of this element is in the cementing together of the plant cells to form the plant body. Growing regions are most affected by deficiency and death results. In soil culture calcium is more important as a soil conditioner and deficiency is seldom encountered, but in solution culture deficiencies do occur.

Magnesium. Though not present throughout the plant body as are those elements just considered, magnesium is a component of the chlorophyll molecule. It has other functions. Magnesium-deficient plants exhibit yellow older leaves (chlorosis) and green young leaves. Chlorosis of the older leaves is not necessarily general, the yellowing occurring between the veins or along the margins.

Sulphur. Though a constituent of certain amino acids (the building blocks of proteins) and necessary to ensure that the proteins adopt the correct molecular configuration, sulphur is also involved in many vital reactions within the plant.

The Trace Elements

Iron. While not a part of the chlorophyll molecule, iron is required to permit the synthesis of this pigment. It would be expected that deficiency would cause chlorosis, and it does, but unlike magnesium deficiency iron deficiency results in the *young* leaves turning yellow. Iron is a constituent part of a number of the catalytic agents (enzymes) which carry out chemical reaction within the cell.

Manganese, Copper, Zinc and Molybdenum. All are associated directly or indirectly with the catalytic agents of metabolism.

Boron. Its exact role is conjectural.

It is not generally realised that the mineral elements just discussed form only a very small part of the plant by weight. The following is an analysis of maize:

TABLE 2

	per cent
Water	75
Organic matter	23
Ash	2
	100

In this case it can be seen that the minerals make up about 2 per cent of the whole. A plant which has a greater water content will have a smaller fraction of the whole made up of mineral matter.

Presenting the facts in another way, it may be said that the plant is 90 per cent water and 10 per cent dry matter. The dry matter is made up of carbon and oxygen (from the atmosphere) and hydrogen (from the water absorbed). About 2 per cent of the dry matter, ie 1/500th of the total weight of the plant, is mineral matter taken up from the soil. It is this which concerns us.

23

The removal of 50 tons of tomatoes from one acre would result in extracting from the soil about 250 lb of minerals. Since the fruit is only part of the plant, the amount that is removed by the crop is larger as we discard the stems and leaves.

The whole subject of nutrition will be dealt with later with more precision.

CHAPTER TWO

Hydroponics:
An introduction

A modern definition might be: 'Hydroponics is the practice of growing plants in a medium, other than soil, using mixtures of essential plant nutrient elements dissolved in water.'

The term 'hydroponics', derived from two Greek words 'hydro' (water) and 'ponos' (labour), was coined by Dr W. F. Gericke of California, who put early laboratory experiments on to a commercial basis. The Californian professor grew tomatoes in solutions of plant nutrient elements in water. His results were highly spectacular. So much so that, after the journalists had exaggerated the facts out of all proportion, every John Citizen was mixing a few cents worth of various chemicals in jars or tins and waiting patiently for the magic spell to begin. Of course more often than not very little happened. This was in the early 1930s.

Shortly after that period, and particularly during the war years, plants were grown in solid media other than soil. The same plant nutrient elements dissolved in water were used, only these were either watered on or pumped into the media at definite periods of time. Although called variously 'aggregate culture', 'soil-less culture', 'nutriculture', or 'chemiculture', Dr Gericke's term is so universally used that *all* forms of growing plants without soil are loosely referred to as 'hydroponics'. In spite of being a misnomer, we shall continue throughout the book with this term.

BRIEF HISTORY

Hydroponics is by no means a new concept. Plant scientists from the beginning of time have been curious to know what composes plants – hence what substances make them grow. It is thought that John Woodward, in England, first unwittingly started the science of hydroponics. This was in 1699. Very probably experiments were made even before that time. Anyway, Woodward cultivated plants in water to which he added different types of garden soil. He thereby showed that certain substances derived from earth, rather than water itself, were responsible for plant growth.

The lead in this field then went over to France, where De Saussure (in 1804) and Boussingault (in 1851–6) both showed that certain substances derived from soil and the gases from the atmosphere were necessary for plants to grow.

The classical experiments of Sachs (1860) and Knop (1861–5) were, however, recognised to be the real beginning of the science of hydroponics. As every student of botany learns, these German plant physiologists were able to grow plants in a mixed solution of simple inorganic salts showing that they were essential plant nutrients. Included in these solutions were salts such as potassium phosphate, calcium sulphate, potassium nitrate, and others (see Chapter 9), and these provided the elements nitrogen, phosphorus, potassium, magnesium, sulphur, calcium, and iron. By using specially purified salts, workers of the twentieth century have increased our knowledge of the plant's nutrient requirements, so that present-day formulations include the trace elements as part of the recipe. Amongst those who have contributed to this knowledge since Sachs and Knop are Tollens (1882), Tottingham (1914), Shive (1915), Hoagland (1919), Trelease (1933), and Arnon (1938). The number of formulae which have been published for general and specialised use is large indeed, but quite satisfactory growth can be obtained using the formulae devised by Sachs and Knop if we now add the trace elements.

Dr Gericke's pioneering work was followed by many enthusiastic amateurs encouraged by sensational press reports of the success of hydroponics in growing bumper crops. Dr Gericke himself grew tomatoes so large that stepladders had to be used to harvest the crop, but the man-in-the-street had as many failures as successes and the growing of plants in culture solution was returned to the laboratories.

However, scientific curiosity was revived during World War II on the basis of experimental work much extended from Dr Gericke's original studies. While most of the work took place in the USA, research stations in other parts of the world were also active.

The health of troops stationed on remote barren islands in the Pacific and other oceans was of prime importance to the Allied command, and as the British navy had learned in the eighteenth century the diet of a fighting man had to include fresh fruit and vegetables if he were to remain healthy. It was decided that these should be available to the soldiers, sailors, and airmen stationed on these inhospitable islands. The only way this could be done was to grow fruit and vegetables by hydroponics. A good example of providing this dietary requirement was seen on Wake Island, the rocky nature of which precluded any normal form of agriculture. Water culture was developed, and from tanks 120 sq ft in area 33 lb of tomatoes, 20 heads of lettuce, 20 lb of string beans, 15 lb of vegetable marrow, and 44 lb of sweet corn were produced weekly.

The US army constructed the world's largest hydroponic installation on Chofu Island, Japan. On this 55-acre site stands a greenhouse covering 232,000 sq ft and containing eighty-seven gravel beds each 300 ft long by 4 ft wide.

Many commercial growers in America prefer this technique for growing floral crops such as carnations, gladioli and chrysanthemums, and several large commercial enterprises practise hydroponics.

In Southern Africa the largest hydroponic installation is in the desert of South West Africa at Oranjemund. Here the Consolidated Diamond Mines Limited annually produces thousands of pounds of fresh lettuces and tomatoes in gravel and in sand.

ADVANTAGES AND DISADVANTAGES

'Why bother with chemicals, tanks and such things, when all

you have to do is to put seed in the ground, water it, and leave the rest to Nature?'

There are several answers to this question:
(1) no need to fertilise (build up the fertility of the soil)
(2) no cultivation;
(3) no crop rotation;
(4) virtually no weeds;
(5) a tendency towards uniform results;
(6) cleanliness;
(7) larger yields;
(8) less labour;
(9) better control;
(10) ease of starting off new plants;
(11) a means of upgrading poor plants.

1. NO NEED TO FERTILISE

There is nothing better for growing plants than a first-class soil. But what makes such a soil? Among the many attributes that such a soil must have is a balanced supply of plant nutrients, but many soils in their natural states are deficient in one or more of the essential plant nutrients. Such deficiencies can be corrected by applying superphosphate and other phosphatic fertilisers to remedy a shortage of phosphorus, potassium chloride or sulphate to correct potassium deficiency, and salts of ammonium or nitrates, or organic nitrogen such as urea, to take care of any lack of nitrogen. No matter how much or how little fertiliser is applied only a portion is used by the plant; a great deal is lost in the drainage waters and by binding in the soil.

In the hydroponic method a balanced composition of totally available plant nutrients is provided. The inconsistencies and uncertainties of fertiliser applications to soil are avoided.

2. NO CULTIVATION

The back-breaking tasks of digging, raking or hoeing are virtually unknown in hydroponics. This is particularly true of the coarser media such as coarse sand or gravel. The voids in gravel provide all the soil atmosphere required by the plant. In fact with the sub-irrigation technique in gravel, this atmosphere is replenished at least once daily. Part of the outstanding success of this method is due to the periodical supply of fresh air to the root system.

3. NO CROP ROTATION

There is no need to practise crop rotation in hydroponics. Lettuce, tomatoes or any other crop can equally well follow a similar crop as not, and often this is desirable. Crop rotations were developed to maintain soil fertility and to check plant diseases caused by soil-borne organisms. With hydroponics the maintenance of fertility is inherent in the system, and since the causal organisms of many plant diseases usually need organic matter to be present in the soil (it is not present in water culture) for their survival, the system can be kept free of these diseases. That does not mean to say that hydroponic culture is free from disease, for the plants are just as subject to the diseases which are caused by air-borne organisms, but it should be remembered that aggregates are generally easier to sterilise effectively.

4. NO WEEDS

More often than not sterile media are used for growing, so the equivalent of 'soil-borne' weeds is unknown.

The odd wind-blown seeds, if they do manage to get a footing, are very easily dealt with.

Imagine gardening with one of its major irritations virtually eliminated!

5. UNIFORM RESULTS

This is a particular boon for the commercial grower, who is, among other things, interested in uniformity of size of bloom or regularity of vegetable production.

Hydroponics is a methodical approach to such production. In fact it may be looked upon as a formularised method of cultivation.

Soils vary tremendously both in their physical and chemical make-up. Results necessarily vary too. With hydroponics gravel may be chosen, as for example a $\frac{1}{16}$ to $\frac{1}{8}$ in sandstone chip. This factor will remain constant. The formulation of the nutrient elements chosen can be retained indefinitely. The climate, of course, will be a variable factor, but even this may be controlled within limits especially in greenhouses.

Once the optimum combination has been arrived at, it can be repeated at will.

6. CLEANLINESS

Many a victim of dysentery rues the day he ate those infected lettuce leaves. This is a very real danger when animal excreta are used for enriching the soil.

The US Army's hydroponic project in Japan was carried out largely for this reason. Many generations of unsanitary cultivation had left the soil so full of disease that the US occupation troops were forbidden to eat fresh soil-grown vegetables.

Sterile gravel and nutrient solutions solved that problem completely. (NB. Some authorities disagree violently with this philosophy.)

7. LARGER YIELDS

Larger yields may be expected, but not spectacularly so. Many people imagine that hydroponic cultivation necessarily implies extraordinary yields.

If 'yield' is defined as the return of fruit or flower per unit growing area per unit time, then the hydroponic method is superior. The reasons for this are not difficult to see. Firstly, plants mature more quickly. Tomatoes, for example, mature within 4 months from time of seeding. Lettuce take about 8-10 weeks. Secondly, since there is no competition by the plants for nutrient, it is possible to plant closer together. Both these factors add up to greater yields.

At the CDM installation at Oranjemund it is commonplace to harvest 1,000 lb of tomatoes per 4 ft x 50 ft gravel tank, ie per

200 sq ft. Growing in each tank area are 99 tomato vines. Reckoning on the basis of 100 tanks to the acre, a yield figure of 50 short tons per acre is arrived at. The farmer who produces 12 tons per acre will indeed be pleased with himself.

With some crops, such as the tomato, it might conservatively be estimated that under smooth working conditions the hydroponic method will produce four to five times the yield expected in soil.

8. LESS LABOUR

It is a well-recognised fact that labour is one of the most expensive items in manufactured goods. The same is true of agriculture. There is digging to be done, fertiliser to be applied, and frequent irrigation. All three operations can be virtually eliminated in the hydroponic method. Dudley Harris's time-clock operated gravel sub-irrigated tank is as near automatic gardening as one can get. Since a very full description of this is given in Chapter Seven, suffice it to say that automation in the hydroponic method is one of its most attractive attributes.

It is actually possible to go on vacation – return home, and pick the flowers or fruit from your tank . . . that is, if you have a friend to adjust the pH of your solution occasionally!

9. BETTER CONTROL

Of the many problems confronting gardeners, perhaps the most frequent is that of pH control. On one occasion a large-scale grower of proteas complained about the death of many of his young seedlings growing in a mixture of Cape Flats (near Cape Town) sand and mountain soil. The pH was found to be 8·0. Proteas, however, thrive in definite acid conditions at pH 4–5. The problem of reducing the pH in soil is not an easy one.

In the hydroponic system this problem is easily dealt with. Since inert growing media are almost exclusively used, it is a relatively simple matter to adjust the pH of the nutrient solution to almost any desired level below 7·0.

It is also comparatively easy to provide more or less nitrogen, phosphorus, potassium, etc, should the plants require special treatment. In general, leaf crops thrive on nitrogen, root crops prefer more phosphorus. With hydroponics this can be arranged.

10. EASE OF STARTING NEW PLANTS

Growing seedlings in materials of high capillarity such as lignite or vermiculite is simplicity itself. There is no necessity to prepare a special soil. Seedlings transplant with a minimum of shock. Both these factors add up to greater efficiency and ease for the gardener.

There is no finer way of revitalising poor plants than by transplanting them from soil into a hydroponic tank. Providing there is no serious damage, a poorly growing plant may be transformed into a vigorous and healthy plant in the tank. It may then be transplanted once again into soil if required. This upgrading procedure is analogous to the process of fattening cattle after they have lost weight as a result of the rigours of transportation.

Most of the advantages just discussed are of particular interest to the commercial grower. However, there are also a few more advantages of special interest to the small-scale grower.

There is a vast and growing population of flat-dwellers in most urban centres and hydroponics is especially suited to these people. Flower-boxes filled with vermiculite and watered with nutrient will grow almost anything the flat-dweller may desire: attractive indoor gardens, window-sill arrangements, balcony vegetables – all are possible with hydroponics.

Finally, mention should be made of hydroponics as an interesting hobby for anyone from 10 years of age upwards. It also affords opportunities for the physically handicapped which conventional gardening methods preclude.

Surely there are disadvantages too.

Here are some of them:

1. On a large scale the initial outlay is comparatively high. Tanks, for example, are made of concrete. There is also ancillary equipment like pumps, reservoirs, and sometimes even glasshouses. This rather limits commercial growing to relatively

high-priced floral crops such as carnations, gladioli, chrysanthemums or attractively wrapped vegetables fetching special prices.

Hydroponics really comes into its own in areas where normal agricultural practice is not possible and transport of fresh produce expensive.

2. Some people state that hydroponics requires a bit of chemical knowledge, which frightens many off.

While it is perfectly true that on a large scale it is useful to have a basic knowledge of agricultural chemistry and plant physiology, the problem of making the plant nutrient is solved by using the commercially available one-powder plant nutrient mixtures. These have all the essential macro and trace elements present in a water-soluble form, and are balanced for general use. The only control necessary is that of pH. They are usually reasonably priced and it is only necessary to know the poundage per week per given tank area to use. The single powder nutrient eliminates the need for chemical knowledge, expensive scales, stocks of chemicals, etc.

33

H—B

CHAPTER THREE

The three different types

It will no doubt be clear by now that hydroponics involves growing plants, in a medium other than soil, by means of a special mixture of fertiliser chemicals.

There are three distinct types of hydroponics, which we may call:

1. Water culture – the true hydroponics of Dr Gericke.

2. Aggregate culture, where a solid *inorganic* medium provides the rooting substrate. Commonly used substrates are sand, gravel, vermiculite, and perlite.

3. Peat culture employing a solid organic medium which is nutritionally inert. The choice of medium is not restricted to peat, though this is the most commonly used. Recent trials have shown that lignite is most satisfactory, and under this heading we can consider growing plants on straw bales. In this last case the medium evenually breaks down and begins to provide plant nutrients, and these can upset the precision of the feeding by solution.

In intensive horticulture the grower often engages in what might be termed hybrid practices. While he uses soil as the rooting medium for his plants the supply of plant nutrients is by the application of nutrient solutions. We shall not consider these hybrid practices.

1. WATER CULTURE – The True 'Hydroponics'
This chapter is really intended to summarise the three main types, but water culture will not be discussed in detail. The

reason is that this is the least adaptable and is not nowadays used to any large extent.

Construction

Tanks of 6–8 in depth and any convenient length and width, but normally not more than 4 ft wide, are used. The material of construction can be glass, plastic, wood, metal or concrete. The last three materials would have to be painted with at least two coats of a bitumen paint or emulsion.

A wire framework, which could be $\frac{1}{4}$ to $\frac{1}{2}$ in mesh bird wire, is supported on a recess near the top of the tank. A bedding of porous material (litter), which can be wood, wool, muslin, peat moss or even rice hulls, is placed over this wire.

The frame is placed over the top of the tank, which is filled with a suitable nutrient solution. It is important to leave an air space of about $\frac{1}{2}$ to 1 in between the bottom of the frame and top of the nutrient solution. As the roots of the plant grow, the volume of the nutrient can be reduced slightly until a 2 in air space exists. This space is necessary for supplying oxygen to the roots of the plant. On a large scale aerators are used to bubble air through the

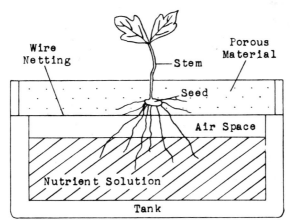

Fig 6 A typical water-culture (hydroponic) tank unit
(after W. F. Gericke)

solution or the latter may be circulated by means of a pump.

Seeds may either be germinated in the litter, which must be kept moist with nutrient during the germination period, or plants may be started elsewhere and transplanted into the frame. Bulbs and tubers may also be directly planted into the litter. It is essential to always keep the litter moist.

From time to time the solution level must be adjusted, either by draining solution from the tank if it is too high, or by adding more nutrient solution or water if the nutrient has become too concentrated. The solution acidity (pH) must be frequently checked.

After 7-10 days the old nutrient solution is replaced by a fresh one.

The details just given refer more particularly to the commercial type of hydroponic tank.

The Home Unit

For the reader who wishes to 'play around' on a small scale there are several attractive devices.

An ordinary fruit jar can serve as the tank or nutrient container. This is fitted with a large cork or even a $\frac{1}{4}$ in wooden cover painted with bitumen. Two holes are bored, one for a plastic or glass tube to aerate the nutrient, the other with a 'keyhole' extension for supporting the plant system. The plant is slid into the 'keyhole' and supported with glass wool packed firmly around (see Fig 7).

In order to keep the light from the roots, it will be necessary either to coat the outside of the jar with a bitumen paint or to wrap brown paper around it.

Use a commercial 'one-powder' nutrient dissolved in water. Alternatively one may be made up from the formulae given in Chapter Nine.

Water culture is somewhat cumbersome and is undoubtedly more difficult for the amateur to master.

The other methods of hydroponic culture are notably more practical.

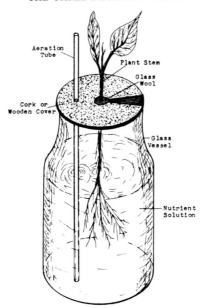

Aeration
Tube

Plant Stem

Glass
Wool

Cork or
Wooden Cover

Glass
Vessel

Nutrient
Solution

Fig 7 The glass jar home
unit

2. (a) SAND, VERMICULITE AND PERLITE CULTURE

This method of hydroponic culture utilises solid inert inorganic media such as sand, vermiculite (a micaceous mineral expanded by heat treatment) or perlite (another mineral treated with heat to make it porous). Sand, unlike the others, does not of itself hold water, retention of water being dependent on the forces of capillarity.

Seeds, or young seedlings, are sown or planted in the moist medium and a suitable nutrient solution used to 'water' the plants. Many schedules are available, depending on the rate and types of growth that is wanted and on the time of year. For vigorous feeders growing rapidly every occasion of watering will be with nutrient solution, but when light is limiting, as in winter, or where less vigorous growth is desired, perhaps only two in seven of the waterings will be with nutrient, the others being with water.

Sprinkling a dry powder nutrient on the surface of the sand,

37

and watering it in constitutes another method of feeding the plants. This method does not provide the fine control that can be achieved by the first one described.

A useful tip when using the above rooting media is to overlay them with about 1 cm (nearly $\frac{1}{2}$ in) of coarse sand or fine gravel. Both vermiculite and perlite have a tendency to displace easily (indeed they will float), and fine sand will compact on watering. The overlay of coarse sand prevents this. The containers used in this technique are standard free-draining plant pots and trays, and one hazard is that when very wet these substrates tend to flow like thin mud through the drainage holes. Some method of preventing this is desirable. Crocks as used in normal potting help, as can putting coarse gravel in the bottom, or covering the holes with nylon gauze. Sub-irrigation can be adopted, but this technique will be better appreciated after reading Section 2 (b).

Since equipment is cheap, and satisfactory results may be obtained for a very small investment, sand or vermiculite culture is recommended for the beginner or flat-dweller. He can purchase very cheaply a tin of hydroponic nutrient powder, some vermiculite, a plastic or asbestos-cement window-box, a few packets of seeds, and a small watering-can. He is then fully equipped to begin soil-less growing.

No technical knowledge is really necessary, and provided he is prepared to respond to the requirements of his plants, the beginner should soon be able to grow a bumper crop of tomatoes in the space of a window-box.

This particular hydroponic method is nearest to growing in soil. Irrigation is usually from above.

2. (b) GRAVEL CULTURE

Gravel culture is the widely used commercial method of hydroponics. Sub-irrigation techniques were developed in conjunction with the use of this substrate for growing plants and the two terms gravel culture and sub-irrigation have become almost interchangeable. The essential feature of sub-irrigation is that the nutrient solution is forced into the gravel from the base

1 *The water-culture of roses*

of the container and gradually floods the bed either partially, not reaching the surface, or completely when liquid is seen at the surface. The liquid is then allowed to drain away. It can be seen that this method has two results: firstly, nutrients are always available, and secondly, the roots are always exposed, except for the short time they are actually in contact with the solution, to an atmosphere which has adequate amounts of oxygen.

The nutrient solution is stored in an external reservoir from where it is pumped into the gravel through a pipe at the end of a waterproof bed (also called a 'tank'). The solution percolates through the gravel. When the pump is switched off, the solution flows back into the reservoir for topping-up and re-use.

The word 'gravel' refers to a *size* not to a *type* of stone. The usual limits are $\frac{1}{16}$ to $\frac{3}{8}$ in.

The gravel must be fine enough to hold sufficient moisture for the requirements of the plants, but at the same time it should be coarse to allow the free drainage of surplus water.

39

One of the merits of the gravel sub-irrigation system is that 'old' air is forced out during pumping and 'fresh' air replaces it during drainage.

Another advantage is that the nutrient is being re-used for as long a period as it can adequately supply the plants' needs. It is then pumped away and replaced with fresh nutrient.

Gravel sub-irrigation is the most efficient type of hydroponics for commercial purposes. In the United States, and several other parts of the world, this type is practised by commercial growers.

Although the most efficient and practical type for commercial conditions, gravel culture at the same time involves the greatest initial outlay. But there is less wastage of water, nutrient chemicals, and greater control of nutrient solution balance. All-important, too, is that labour requirements are less. By means of time-clocks, electric pumps may be automatically switched on and off.

Perhaps the greatest advantage of gravel culture is that it is an improved forcing method of growth of great value to floriculturists.

3. PEAT CULTURE (INCLUDING LIGNITE)

While peat has been used for a large number of years as an ingredient in compost, its widespread use as the only component of a rooting medium is relatively recent. One of the disadvantages attending the use of peat is its variability, but as more investigations are made into this substance, consistency can be obtained by suitable blending and prior trials by the suppliers. In many parts of the world a supply of peat is more readily available than that of even a mineral like sand. The great value of peat is its moisture-holding capacity, and it also has a degree of tolerance of imbalance that the other media mentioned do not possess. It is light and pleasant to handle (whereas vermiculite and perlite, while light, can be unpleasant to handle, especially the latter), and can be stored in plastic bags, which may be used as containers in which the plants can be grown.

Commercial mixtures of peat and vermiculite are available, but the mixture does not necessarily have better properties than the

*2 Hydroponics trough being charged with
Kapag lignite*

3 Mock-up of corner of hydroponics trough

straight materials. Often these mixtures have plant nutrients added and all the grower need do is add water after planting out. This results in an activity no different than if soil were used.

Large-scale use of peat is likely in the temperate zones where there are adequate supplies. Other organic deposits can be used and, as we have said, lignite is showing promise. There is also the prospect that suitably devised synthetic materials will cease to be a curiosity and find widespread use as rooting media. Poly-ether, polyester, and polystyrene foams possess the necessary physical properties of the ideal rooting medium, but the chemicals which are added to obtain these properties often are harmful to roots. If the demand were there the chemical industry would, however, solve the problems.

CHAPTER FOUR

Hydroponics for the small-scale grower

All hydroponic methods, on a small scale, involve filling some type of *container* with the *growing medium, planting the seeds* (or transplanting the seedlings), and *watering* the medium with the *nutrient solution*.

THE CONTAINER

This can be made of any suitable material such as asbestos-cement, wood, plastic, earthenware, metal or even glass. The depth should be about 8–9 in for most crops, though for potatoes a depth of 12 in is preferable.

PAINTING

For various reasons it is usual to paint the inside surfaces of the container with a bitumen paint. In the case of asbestos-cement, its alkalinity would upset the balance of the nutrient solution; with wood, bitumen paint helps to prevent rotting; a galvanised metal surface is painted to prevent solution of the zinc, which in excess amounts is toxic to plants. Plastic surfaces need not be painted. If glass is used, it must be painted on the outside in order to prevent light falling on the roots in the medium within.

A bitumen paint is obtainable in small amounts from most paint or hardware shops. Those who require large quantities can purchase it from the oil companies. Always ensure that the paint bought is not derived from *coal-tar,* as this substance (often sold as a bitumen paint) can contain traces of materials toxic to plants. A petroleum-based bitumen is what is required.

DRAINAGE

Except when sub-irrigation is practised, all containers must be provided with drainage holes in their base.

Efficient drainage is of such vital importance that it is worth emphasising, thus:

EFFICIENT DRAINAGE

This should be a self-evident fact, but it is often neglected by people practising hydroponics. The reason for perfect drainage should be clear after reading Chapter One, where the importance of air (oxygen) to the roots was discussed.

It is essential when growing in soil to dig and turn it from time to time. In hydroponics we also strive to attain a well-aerated medium. Good drainage is a first step in this direction.

Usually $\frac{1}{4}$ in holes drilled into the base or sides of the container are quite sufficient. Flat-dwellers need only ask the hardware store, where the window-box was purchased, to drill the required five or six holes for them. Those with brace-and-bits or electric drills may prefer to do their own drilling.

To prevent the medium falling through the holes, stick on 1 sq in of nylon gauze as a filter. This is best done while the bitumen paint is still tacky. Nylon gauze is obtainable at almost any hardware store. A piece may even be lying around the house. It is used extensively for curtaining and dress materials. About $\frac{1}{16}$ in mesh is suitable. The reason for using nylon gauze is that it is virtually indestructible. Cotton gauze is easily decomposed under the constantly moist conditions. The other synthetics such as orlon, terylene, etc, are just as suitable.

After the paint has dried for at least 24 hr (or less, if it has been standing in the sun), place about a 1 in layer of drainage stones, $\frac{1}{4}$ or $\frac{1}{2}$ in in diameter, in the bottom of the container. These stones can be of practically any mineral composition, such as granite, sandstone or shale, but do not use any stone that will react with the nutrient solution or is likely to contain toxic materials. An example of the former is limestone or builders' rubble; of the latter, coal cinders. Most householders should have no difficulty in procuring suitable stones, though it might present a problem for the flat-dweller.

THE MEDIUM

The two media which are in common use are builders' sand and vermiculite. Gravel may also be used if desired, but discussion of this medium will form the main subject-matter of Chapters Seven and Eight. Let us confine ourselves for the moment to the two well-known and well-used media – sand and vermiculite.

(a) Sand

This is a very variable material indeed. Like gravel, sand can vary in size, shape, composition, and colour. Anything from $\frac{1}{100}$ in to $\frac{1}{10}$ in may be described as sand. Particles may be angular or rounded. Calcareous (lime-containing) minerals, such as shell, may be present or the sand may be contaminated with silt or organic matter.

The best sand to use is a washed river sand ranging from $\frac{1}{10}$ to $\frac{1}{40}$ in in diameter. More often than not, this is difficult to obtain in small quantities.

Builders' sand is often suitable and almost universally obtainable. Some builders' sands, however, contain quantities of shell or other calcareous matter which will upset the pH value of the nutrient solution.

Large or commercial-scale growers may pre-treat a calcareous sand by soaking it overnight in a strong superphosphate solution. This is not practicable on a small scale, however. After treatment the shell particles are coated with a layer of tricalcium phosphate which inactivates them towards the nutrient solution for some time.

A simple test to determine whether a sand contains shell or not is to place a $\frac{1}{4}$ in layer of this medium in a glass tumbler, just cover with water, and add an equal volume of hydrochloric acid (obtainable from your pharmacist). A slight to vigorous effervescence indicates small to large amounts of shell.

(b) Vermiculite

This is a mica mineral – a complex hydrated magnesium aluminium iron silicate in chemical composition. It exists naturally in plates or lamellae, which are exceedingly thin.

This mineral is mined in South Africa and the USA. The main use after it has been expanded by heat is as fire-resistant insulation in buildings. It is almost completely inert and does not sustain rodents or pests, hence its popularity for this purpose. While large quantities are used in this way not all produced for insulation can be used in horticulture.

To produce horticultural vermiculite it is necessary to locate a deposit which when suspended in water will give a nearly neutral pH (see Chapter Eight), and which does not contain extractable amounts of fluorine or boron, both of which are toxic to plants if present at levels beyond that which the plant will tolerate. Most industrial vermiculites give a pH value greater than 9 and are thus unsuitable for horticultural use, but fortunately there are deposits which give a nearly neutral pH.

The mined mineral is first milled and screened to a size suitable for growing purposes. It is then placed in a furnace at nearly 2,000° F, when a change takes place known as *exfoliation*. In this process the water of hydration is instantaneously turned into steam which forces the hundreds of lamellae outwards concertina-wise. The original particle finally expands to about twelve times its normal thickness.

Hundreds of flat air-cells are thus created. The end product has the properties of absorbence, lightness (about 7 lb per cu ft), bad conductivity (good insulation), and sterility.

Freshly exfoliated vermiculite, therefore, is a useful growing medium for hydroponics, being ideal for the flat-dwellers and householders who have no easy access to other media.

Vermiculite, however, has certain disadvantages. When fresh and full of air cells this medium works well. After periods of use, wear and tear collapse the air cells and the material tends to revert physically to its natural form. Put more simply, the lamellae flake away and can form with water a rather pulpy mass or 'porridge'. This is particularly true of areas receiving constant rainfall. For outdoor commercial establishments, therefore, vermiculite cannot be recommended as a successful growing medium, unless the grower is prepared to renew it at approximately 18 month intervals.

Another disadvantage is the difficulty of chemical sterilisation of old vermiculite. With gravel, sterilisation and subsequent washing present no difficulties. Due to its great absorbent properties, the same cannot be said of vermiculite.

In windy areas the light particles of vermiculite on the surface tend to be rather easily blown about. It is claimed that this difficulty can be overcome by mixing with sand, but owing to the difference in their bulk densities (vermiculite 7 lb: sand 90 lb per cu ft) these two materials do not mix at all well. The authors would like to make a point of discouraging any grower from attempting to mix vermiculite with other harder media. This applies particularly to sand whose relatively hard particles only hasten the break up of the air cells of vermiculite leading to the 'porridge' condition mentioned above.

Exfoliated vermiculite has rather paradoxical properties as the following comparison shows:

TABLE 3

Advantages	Disadvantages
1. High absorbency; holds moisture on dry, hot days.	Holds too much moisture for wet climatic conditions.
2. Exfoliation means aeration, ie oxygen for the roots.	Lamellae flake away with excess moisture, wear and tear, leading to exclusion of oxygen.
3. Freshly prepared vermiculite is sterile.	Cannot be easily re-sterilised on site owing to difficulty of washing out excess chemicals.
4. Very light in bulk, easily handled.	Lightness is a disadvantage in windy areas.

Vermiculite is an ideal medium for raising seedlings, however. Here its 'warmness', due to its property of good insulation, is a distinct advantage for germinating seeds. This will form the subject matter of Chapter Six.

To summarise, vermiculite is eminently suitable for

(*i*)   flat-dwellers who wish to practice hydroponics in pots or window-boxes, whether indoors or on balconies,

(*ii*) all gardeners who wish to have an almost foolproof, effective method of raising seedlings for their garden or hydroponic tank,

(*iii*) the gardener who wishes to operate only on a small scale in his backyard.

It is definitely not recommended as a medium for the commercial grower of flowers or vegetables.

Contrary to belief: VERMICULITE HAS NO FOOD VALUE.

While for all practical purposes this statement is true, it is not quite technically correct. It has been suggested that some of the magnesium forming the complex structure of vermiculite is leached out by the water and becomes available to the plant.

In recent years vermiculite has been in short supply, resulting in much higher costs, especially in the UK.

(*c*)   *Perlite*

Perlite, essentially a mined mineral of the potassium sodium aluminium silicate composition, finds extensive horticultural use in the United States. Commercially available as Peralite, it is obtainable in Great Britain from British Gypsum.

For horticultural purposes, the natural mineral is screened and processed by heating to 1,700°F, which creates countless tiny bubbles in a glass-like surface. It is marketed in both fine and coarse grades. The latter is about 1–3 mm in size and weighs 80–110 kg per cu/m. Perlite is soft and, unless carefully handled, will powder if rubbed between the fingers. Being predominantly white, algal growth is encouraged.

Perlite is an excellent medium for germinating seeds or

striking cuttings in hydroponics. It is superior to vermiculite owing to its greater physical stability.

It gives an almost neutral pH in distilled water.

The coarser grade of perlite finds use as a type of gravel in hydroponics.

(d) Lignite

Several deposits of lignite or brown coal exist, the most readily available source in the UK being Devon. Lignite is organic in origin and has the following analysis:

Typical ultimate analysis (per cent)		Typical mineral analysis (per cent)	
Carbon	46·7	Resin & Tannins	approx 12
Hydrogen	3·5	Fats and Waxes	approx 2
Nitrogen	0·5	Humic Acid	approx 12
Sulphur	3·2	Lignite	approx 46
Oxygen	18·3	Cellulose	less than 1
Ash	27·8	Mineral Matter	approx 27

Its chief virtue for hydroponics is its high capillarity or absorbency, enabling it to be used in trenches and pots with drainage holes 2– 3 in from the base, so that a permanent store of moisture nutrients can be absorbed by capillary pull. Although organic,

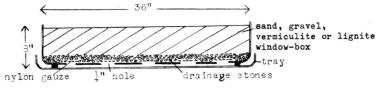

Fig 8 Cross-section of a window-box

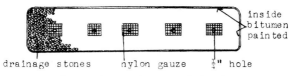

Fig 9 Bird's-eye view of a window-box

49

lignite breaks down slowly, giving the best of both worlds between the use of an inert medium (of little or no capillarity) and a soft rapidly decomposing organic medium such as peat (which can give rise to considerable nutritional problems). In essence, however, it is used in a similar manner to peat, although nutrition is much more straightforward.

PREPARATION OF WINDOW-BOXES

The stage-by-stage preparation of a window-box, for example the asbestos-cement type of dimensions 36 in $\times$ 8 in $\times$ 8 in (see Figs 8 and 9) will now be described.

Step 1

Drill five or six $\frac{1}{4}$-in holes in the bottom of the window-box. These can be zigzagged over the bottom if desired.

Step 2

Paint the inside surface of the box with bitumen paint. If one coat is insufficient, apply a second coat. Allow to dry thoroughly. Ensure that drainage holes are not blocked with paint.

Step 3

Cut 1 in squares of nylon curtain net and, while the paint is still tacky, place a square over each hole in the inside bottom of the window-box. The paint must be given sufficient time to dry *thoroughly*.

Step 4

Place a 1 in layer of drainage stones, about $\frac{1}{4}$ or $\frac{1}{2}$ in in diameter, over the bottom of the box.

Step 5

Pour in sufficient builders' sand or *horticultural* grade of vermiculite or lignite to fill the box to within $\frac{1}{2}$ in of the top.

The window-box is now ready for watering and planting of seeds, cuttings or bulbs.

Earthenware, asbestos-cement or plastic pots are prepared in a similar manner. In the case of plastic, however, it is not necessary to paint the inside with bitumen. Only a single $\frac{1}{2}$ in hole need be drilled in the bottom of pots.

Tin cans may also be used for hydroponics. Their preparation follows the pattern described for pots or window-boxes, but if a sub-irrigation system is used a series of $\frac{1}{8}$ in holes punched in the sides and near the bottom of the can is very effective.

The chief disadvantage of using tin cans is that corrosion of the metal sooner or later takes place. The life of the can may be prolonged by two or three coats of bitumen paint inside and out. The chief advantage is cheapness.

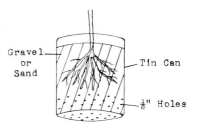

Fig 10 *The tin-can method*

Other containers such as shallow wooden boxes, old motor battery cases, guttering, even cattle-troughs, may be adapted as containers for hydroponics. Always try to arrange for a growing depth of about 8–9 in. With lignite, make drainage holes 2–3 in from base in side of container.

PLANTING THE SEEDS IN THE MEDIUM

The details for raising seedlings form the subject matter of Chapter Six, so only brief mention will be made here.

Returning to the step-by-step summary above, continue as follows:

Step 6

By means of a watering can or the fine spray of a garden hose, sprinkle *tap water* over the surface of the medium until the whole mass is saturated and water drips *freely* from the holes in the bottom or sides of the container.

Step 7

(For direct sowing of seeds.) Allow the excess water to drain away for a few minutes. With a small stick or sharp end of a pencil 'draw' parallel trenches about $\frac{1}{4}$ in deep and 2 in apart (the depth depending on the size of the seed to be planted) into the surface of the moist medium.

51

Step 8

Place the seeds in the trenches at depths recommended for normal soil planting. Very generally these should be about two or three times the diameter of the seed deep. Larger seeds, like beetroot, should be planted about $\frac{1}{2}$ in deep; while smaller seeds, like celery, should be planted at about $\frac{1}{4}$ in. Some seeds may be planted individually with the aid of a moistened matchstick or camel-hair brush.

Step 9

After sowing the seeds, fill in over the trenches with the medium. Sprinkle lightly with water to allow the seed to settle in. Do not firm down with the hand.

Very small seeds, eg petunia, antirrhinum, etc, may be sown directly, after completing Step 6, by putting them in a pepper-pot and deftly sprinkling them over the surface of the moist medium. With a little practice a nice 'spread' will result. Sprinkle a thin layer of *dry* medium over the scattered seeds and lightly water in.

TRANSPLANTING SEEDLINGS INTO THE MEDIUM

Seedlings may be raised *externally* in seed-beds or seed-trays of soil, sand or vermiculite. The flat-dweller may prefer to buy his seedlings from a garden store or from the many individuals and firms advertising seedlings in the local newspaper. Although it is much more fun raising one's own seedlings either by hydroponics or in soil, there are many people who prefer to purchase them.

Two situations may arise:

(*a*) sometimes the seedlings may have to be transplanted from one medium, which may be sand, vermiculite or perhaps soil, into a different medium;

(*b*) or there is the easier task of transplanting from one medium into the same medium.

The most likely instance of case (*a*) is the transplanting of seedlings from soil into sand, vermiculite or lignite. It is advisable to gently wash away excess soil adhering to the rootlets, being extremely careful not to damage them. Place the whole root system into suitably sized holes. Replace the medium around the plant and gently firm in with the fingers. Space the plants as you would in soil. A 36in window-box, for example, could take three tomato seedlings. It would be cramping them by planting four. With lettuce seedlings you could manage four plants, perhaps five with a squeeze. The only real limitation to the number of plants is light. In the hydroponic system there is virtually no competition for plant food.

Another instance of case (a) is the transplanting of seedlings from vermiculite into sand, gravel or lignite. After removing the seedlings with the aid of a spoon, very gently shake off *some* of the *excess* vermiculite adhering to the rootlets. Place in holes made in the sand, gravel or lignite and gently firm around with the fingers.

The most likely instance of case (b) is the transplanting of seedlings from vermiculite seed-trays into vermiculite window-boxes or larger vessels.

It is only necessary to remove the seedling, with the aid of a spoon, and place the whole clod into a suitable hole made in the surface of the vermiculite.

If seedlings are brought on in either vermiculite or perlite, an excellent method of removing them before pricking off or planting out is to place the seed-tray or pot in a larger container which can hold water and fill this until its water level is just above the surface of the vermiculite or perlite. After a moment or two the seedlings can be removed by gently pulling on the seed leaves. Larger plants can be grasped by the basal part of the stem and gently eased upwards. Done carefully there is no damage to the root hairs, and seedlings so transplanted suffer little, if any, check.

BULBS, CORMS, TUBERS

Planting bulbs, corms, or tubers presents no difficulties. Treat them in the same way as you would in soil, remembering, though, that the only competition is for light.

CUTTINGS

Cuttings root freely in sand and should be treated in as similar a manner as you would treat them in soil. Carnation cuttings are usually rooted in a fine sand by a method which is virtually a hydroponic one.

Many pot-plants, such as African violet, are rooted by leaf-cuttings in either sand or vermiculite. Place the petiole of the leaf in the moist medium and water with half-strength nutrient solution until the rooted cutting is ready for transplanting.

THE PLANT FOOD

Up to this point the preparation and filling of a window-box for hydroponics has not deviated very much from ordinary gardening procedure. The only real difference is that, instead of natural soil, a chemically inert growing medium has been employed.

But now there is an important parting of the ways. In soil it is only necessary to provide sufficient water for the plant to live and develop normally; with hydroponics, in addition to the water, a balanced 'diet' of plant elements vital to growth has to be supplied. This is the *nutrient solution*, also sometimes referred to as the *plant nutrient*, the *mineral elements* or, just simply called the *plant food*.

MAKING THE NUTRIENT SOLUTION

Perhaps an obstacle the man in the street encounters with hydroponics is (so he thinks) his lack of knowledge of chemistry.

The authors would like to assure their readers that this is not so. It is true that, while chemical knowledge is useful, particularly to commercial growers, it is by no stretch of the imagination a *sine qua non* of success.

With the advent of the modern commercial formulae this problem (supposed ignorance of chemical matters) is a thing of the past.

A commercial hydroponic nutrient, available at most horticultural stores, is a powder which has been specially formulated

54

for hydroponic growing. This means that it contains nitrogen, phosphorus, potassium, calcium, magnesium, sulphur, plus the essential trace elements in balanced proportions known to be optimum for general growing. There are many commercial feeds either solid or liquid, which are marketed for plants growing in soil or compost. A knowledge of the mineral requirements of plants will permit you to decide whether these might be used as the source of a hydroponic solution. Some are suitable, some are not; the most obvious omission from those which are unsuitable is calcium. Nearly always the other major elements are present and some are well formulated with the trace elements.

It is far easier for the flat-dweller or householder, with a window-box or two, to purchase a pound of such a powder rather than to buy some twelve or thirteen separate chemicals and compound these himself. For the more scientifically minded, however, Chapter Nine deals with the preparation of chemical formulae.

It is only necessary to dissolve the powder in water and store the solution in a suitable container. Leave standing overnight. Ignore the small sediment remaining at the bottom as all the necessary plant food will have been dissolved by this time. Store the clear solution for future use preferably in glass or polythene containers.

The reason for allowing the solution to stand overnight is that certain constituents of these commercial powders, being less soluble in water than others, require a longer period to dissolve.

It is also important to store the solution in containers protected from the light, which slowly throws iron out of solution. Half- or one-gallon polythene vessels, obtainable at many hardware dealers, are eminently suitable for both mixing and storing the solution. Five-gallon vessels are also available for larger capacities. Metal, almost invariably galvanised, is not to be recommended, unless adequately bitumenised, owing to the solubility of zinc and its toxicity in excess to plants.

For hydroponic growing on a very limited scale, the familiar 26-fluid ounce bottle can serve as a handy container. There are six of these to the imperial gallon. To make one bottleful, dissolve, in water, $\frac{3}{8}$ or $\frac{1}{2}$ *level* teaspoon of most hydroponic nutrient powders. This should last several pot plants at least a week. A half-dozen of these bottles can easily be stored away in a handy cupboard.

Various strengths of solution may be used – weaker for young plants, especially in poor light conditions, stronger for more mature plants.

It is inadvisable to use solutions at concentrations greater than 'full-strength'. The reason for this is given in Chapter One (see plasmolysis). Some people tend to use nutrient solutions stronger than 'full-strength' in the mistaken belief that the plants will grow more quickly! Makers' advice should always be adhered to.

FEEDING THE PLANTS

A suitable container has been selected and prepared, seeds planted or some seedlings transplanted, and the nutrient solution made up. Only one stage remains: to feed (irrigate) the plants.

There are three different methods of irrigation available to the hydroponic grower. These are:

(1) overhead watering,
(2) dry feeding, and
(3) sub-irrigation.

Although this last method is commonly used with the larger tanks, it will nevertheless be described here for it can also be successfully employed on a small scale.

(1) *Overhead watering*

This is about the most straightforward method there is for irrigating several pot plants, window-boxes or seed-trays. Place the nutrient solution in a watering can fitted with a fine rose and sprinkle the solution over the seedlings or growing plants until the medium is *nicely* moist. This means that the medium should be in a condition similar to a *wetted sponge which has just been*

4 *Sansevieras dry-fed in washed sea sand*

wrung out. It does not matter if the foliage is wetted by the nutrient solution provided no greater than maximum concentration is being used. Indeed, with materials such as 'Maxicrop' it is an advantage to apply it to the foliage, as the plant readily absorbs the nutrients through its leaves.

The frequency of irrigation is perhaps the most difficult factor to determine. It would be rather naive to say, 'let experience be your guide'. In the last analysis this is really the answer to the question, but here are some additional pointers:

(a) Sand

Coarser sand usually has to be irrigated once daily in summer. The limiting factor will be the dryness of the sand or, in other words, when water is needed we give nutrient solution. No harm will be done if plain tap water is given instead of nutrient solution occasionally, say at every fourth irrigation. A fine sand may require irrigation every second day in summer and only once or twice a week during the winter months.

The frequency of feeding will depend on many other factors, such as the humidity, presence or absence of wind, type of plant being grown (leafy, eg lettuce; or otherwise, eg carnation), stage of growth, size of container in relation to the plants being grown, size and shape of medium (eg rounded or angular sand), whether under cover or out of doors, etc.

The reader will now more readily appreciate the earlier remarks about experience being the best guide.

(b) Vermiculite, lignite, perlite

Due to their large capacity for holding moisture, these media require less frequent irrigation than others. After the initial soaking described in Step 6 above, it is only necessary to water about every second day in summer while the plants are still young. In winter once or twice a week should be sufficient. These instructions apply to young plants under normal conditions. If it is noticed that the plants are showing signs of wilt during the hotter part of the day through wind, heat or other causes, it probably means that the water supply is low and more should be applied in the form of nutrient solution.

In hot climates, where the nitrogen demand of the plants is likely to be higher than normal, more frequent applications of nutrient solution will have to be given.

For amateurs the technique of using fresh solution of normal strength every time moisture is needed is recommended.

With overhead watering the excess nutrient runs to waste, no attempt being made to collect it. For the small-scale grower it is not worth trying to collect or re-use the nutrient solution, but on a commercial scale this is an important factor in the economics of the hydroponic installation. The sub-irrigation method allows of constant re-use of nutrient.

(2) Dry feeding

As the name implies, food is given to the plants not as a solution in water but in the form of a dry powder. In other words the dry nutrient chemicals are spread over the surface of the medium and lightly watered in.

After the seedlings have appeared (or if seedlings have been transplanted) apply a pinch of powder along the rows or around each plant. Simply water in. The nutrient should last for about 2 weeks. Give the beds, pots or window-boxes a sprinkling of water as often as is necessary to keep them moist between feeds. Avoid overwatering.

In rainy weather it may become necessary to apply plant food at weekly intervals. As in overhead watering, experience is the best guide.

The dry-feed system is definitely the easiest and least expensive method of practising hydroponics on a small scale. It does, however, suffer from one big disadvantage. In some instances it is quite easy to apply the dry powder around the plants. In others, for example with lettuce, it is extremely difficult to do this because of the low-lying leafy nature of the plant. On a small scale this is not so important, but with large-scale growing this objection is a very real one.

A further disadvantage is that the dry-feed system is wasteful of plant food chemicals, especially in comparison with the sub-irrigation technique. However, these are minor disadvantages as far as the householder or flat-dweller is concerned. In fact, for the flat-dweller the dry-feed system avoids the necessity of making up and storing nutrient solutions.

Normal dosage for dry feeding is *about* ½ oz per sq yd. For a 4 in pot use a small pinch of powder sprinkled around the plant. For 9 in pots use no more powder than would thinly cover a 5p coin. A 36 in × 8 in window-box would need about a teaspoonful.

Should these quantities prove inadequate to meet the requirements of the plants, increase the amounts or make more frequent applications.

To beautify your home, you may grow many charming indoor plants like African violet, cyclamen, coleus, amaryllis and so forth, in sand, vermiculite or lignite, using the dry-feed system.

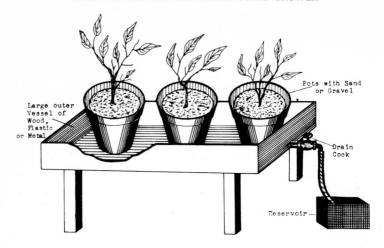

Fig 11 *Sub-irrigation in a larger vessel*

(3) *Sub-irrigation*

The nutrient solution is led in at the bottom of the container, brought to a certain level and allowed to flow back again into the nutrient reservoir. The used solution is topped up with water if necessary and re-used for 10 days to 2 weeks.

This method is particularly effective with gravel. A medium sand may be sub-irrigated, but not vermiculite, because of its rather high water-holding capacity.

The success of the method is largely due to the fact that old air is displaced during irrigation to be replaced by fresh air when the liquid drains out of the medium.

(*a*) *Earthenware pots, tins cans, and other small containers*

To irrigate, place the container in a large outer vessel. Pour in sufficient nutrient solution to half submerge the container. The solution will rise slowly through the drainage holes in the bottom of the sand-filled container. Leave 20 or 30 min. Now completely drain the larger vessel through a tap or by siphon, allowing the nutrient solution to return to its reservoir. Feed once a day in normal summer weather, re-using the solution collected in the reservoir. Add fresh water occasionally to make up that lost by evaporation. Replace with a new batch of solution every 10 days (Fig 11).

(b) *Window-boxes and larger containers*

The method of feeding may be likened to the application of an enema.

The watertight growing container is fitted at one end near the bottom with a small inlet pipe of about $\frac{1}{2}$ in diameter. Attached to this pipe is a short length of plastic or rubber hose which fits over a similar pipe fixed to the bottom of a bucket or 4 gallon oil-can. It should be mentioned here that the size of the reservoir is limited by the ability of the grower to lift weights. A 4 gallon container filled with solution will weigh 40 lb. This seems to be the convenient upper limit of hand-operated sub-irrigated tanks. Above this size hand irrigation becomes cumbersome. The use of light block and tackle might even be considered.

As a square foot of growing area requires about 2 gallons of nutrient solution to irrigate it, the hand method more or less confines the grower to 2 sq ft, which is only a little larger than a 36 in $\times$ 8 in window-box.

With an electric pump the size of the container or tank is practically unlimited.

In order not to disturb the medium during irrigation, a length of half-round tiles or a U-trough is placed on the bottom over the length of the container. The latter is prepared in exactly the same manner described for the window-box above (see Steps 4 and 5).

For irrigation, the nutrient solution in the can is led into the medium by raising the can above the level of the container. Solution will flow into the medium by gravity. When the level of the solution in the container is about an inch from the surface of the medium, the can is returned to the floor, when all excess liquid drains back into it. In order to avoid any fine material clogging the inlet pipe, a small square of nylon gauze can be fitted round it to act as a filter (Fig 12). The same nutrient solution is used over again for about 10 days. Fresh water may be added

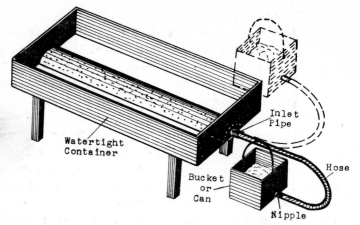

Fig 12 *The 'enema' system of sub-irrigation*

occasionally to make up for evaporation. Outstanding results with a wide variety of flowers and vegetables are obtained by this method.

Daily irrigation in summer weather is again the recommended procedure, although there can be no rules, as the weather varies considerably. Occasional watering from above with fresh tap water is good growing practice to wash out surplus salts.

The prospective small-scale hydroponic grower has now been taken through the various stages of preparation of container, selection of growing medium, seeding, transplanting and, finally, irrigating the plants. Nevertheless there still remain several other points for discussion, namely, the following:

(1) Light requirements.
(2) Rain.
(3) Wilting.
(4) Flushing.
(5) Algae.
(6) Staking.
(7) Wind.
(8) Water.

(1) *Light requirements*

This is a most important consideration. Many growers make the mistake of trying to grow plants on steps or window-sills where the light duration or intensity, or both, is hopelessly inadequate. Naturally the light requirement of different plant types varies. An indoor plant such as coleus needs less light than the tomato. Indoor plants may be grown in a living-room or in the shade of a veranda with perfect success. The African violet prefers a diffused sunlight and high humidity similar to its natural condition in the tropical forests of Central Africa. The first rule, therefore, is to find an aspect suited to the plant being grown. It is quite useless, for example, trying to grow zinnias in the lounge. In searching for the light the plants are sure to grow tall and etiolated.

(2) *Rain*

Large raindrops falling on vermiculite are likely to disturb its surface, perhaps uprooting seedlings. Generally, however, rain will do no harm unless prolonged and violent. In either case some sort of shelter will have to be provided for the plants.

Where outdoor culture is concerned, should the rainfall continue for a week or more, employ the dry-feed system until drier weather returns.

With the sub-irrigation system, when the reservoir has been filled, the draining rain water will have to be run to waste.

(3) *Wilting*

Temporary wilting is usually a sign of insufficient moisture in the medium. This may occur for various reasons. It often happens during the hottest part of the day when transpiration is excessive and moisture in the medium falls to a low level. The remedy is to add water or nutrient solution immediately.

Constant daily wilting in hot weather points to too small a container, eg a tomato plant growing in a small pot. It is advisable to replace this with a larger pot.

Prolonged wilting can lead to permanent damage to the plant and should thus be avoided.

A frequent and more permanent wilt may be the result of other factors. Wilts are diseases to which tomatoes are prone. Root rot is another cause. In fact prolonged or permanent wilting is usually symptomatic of a more serious complaint and should be investigated immediately.

(4) Flushing

Every 6 weeks flood the medium thoroughly from above with fresh water. This will wash out any accumulation of unused salts. Recommence normal feeding as soon as possible.

(5) Algae

Sometimes a green scum appears on the surface of the medium, due to the growth of algae. These are lower forms of plant life which grow on nutrient solutions in the presence of light. Apart from their objectionable appearance, no real harm is done to the plants.

Vermiculite that is too moist or badly drained will almost certainly support algal growth. Although this is rather difficult to counter, one possible remedy is to place a layer of $\frac{1}{2}$ in stones over the surface of the medium. This serves to cut down the light. The plants must be allowed to reach a reasonable height before putting down the stones. Algaecides are now available to control algal growth.

(6) Staking

With pots and window-boxes, particularly those filled with vermiculite, the problem of staking is a very real one. With sand it is possible to sink a wooden stake into the medium, but vermiculite is too soft and affords little support. In this case some system of external staking will have to be devised. The same is true of lignite.

(7) Wind

Wind is very much bound up with the question of staking. Naturally, in windy areas it would be impossible to grow any of the taller plants such as dahlia, tomato, antirrhinum or carnation unless adequate protection from wind blast can be contrived. Staking is essential. Without cutting down their light, it might even become necessary to provide a windbreak for the plants. On a large scale this problem is easier to deal with.

(8) *Water*

This will be considered in detail later. Suffice it to say that most municipal tap waters will be found suitable for making up the nutrient solution. Very brackish waters or extremely 'hard' waters should be avoided. If no other source is available, collected rain-water can always be used.

H—C

CHAPTER FIVE

Simple hydroponic systems

There has been earlier reference to the dry-feed system of hydroponics, which is of course a much simpler system and involves
much less equipment than other systems involving tanks or
troughs. Now in the early 1970s simple dry- and liquid-feed
systems are becoming very popular, particularly when soil
conditions are unsuitable or there is no suitable soil at all under
glass, the existing soil being 'sick' through a build-up of pests
and diseases and accumulation of salts and plant toxins. The
following account deals broadly with simple systems both for
outdoor and greenhouse culture.

CONSTRUCTION OF BEDS

(1) Trenches can be dug out from 1 ft to 4 ft wide and any
convenient length (they can also be wider), and approximately
10–14 in deep. Out of doors a sunny situation should be selected,
while in the greenhouse the most convenient layout of beds
should be employed. It is important to check that drainage is
adequate.

(2) Surround the dug-out area with some material which will
separate it from the soil. Any suitable material may be used;
eg wood, asbestos-cement, galvanised iron, bricks, etc. It would
advisable to apply two coats of a bitumen paint in the case of the
first two materials.

If it has been decided to use wood, cut pieces of timber at
least $\frac{1}{2}$ in thick and of sufficient length to line the outside of the
dug-out area. The width of the timber should be at least 12 in.

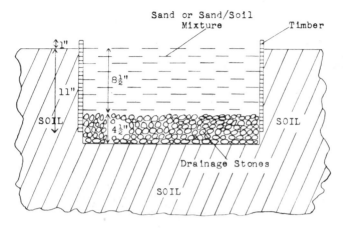

Fig 13 *Dry-feed arrangement in cross-section*

Put the pieces of wood in place around the area so that about $\frac{1}{2}$ to 1 in is above ground level and the rest below. (See Fig 13.)

It will be necessary to support the structure by knocking sections of metal piping or thick wooden stakes into the ground at suitable intervals. For extra support, cross-braces of wood may also have to be nailed across the sides. If desired, the timber may be placed so that half, or even all of it, is above ground level. In the latter case it will be essential to support the structure at frequent intervals.

(3) Place a $4\frac{1}{2}$ in layer of stones, at least $1\frac{1}{2}$ in in diameter, on to the bottom of the structure. These are for drainage. Pieces of broken brick, or almost any material non-toxic to plants may be used.

On top of the drainage stones place an $8\frac{1}{2}$ in layer of the medium. This should consist of builders' sand or a 50–50 mixture of soil and sand. Unless the grower is prepared to replace it at intervals, it is not advisable to choose vermiculite as a growing medium. In hot, dry areas, if no other medium is available, vermiculite has certain advantages, and lignite can also be used. Sea sand, though not recommended, can also be used if the salts are thoroughly washed out with water.

5 *The weekly feed*

(4) Before planting, sprinkle the fertiliser in a thin layer over the surface of the medium. As a guide, roughly $\frac{1}{2}$ to $\frac{3}{4}$ oz per sq yd is about the correct amount to use. Water in thoroughly, using a garden hose. Some lime may also be necessary to adjust the pH figure to between 6 and 7.

Plant the seeds or transplant the seedlings in exactly the same manner as in soil. The only limitation is light. The plants will receive all necessary food from their periodic dry feeds.

FEEDING

If seeds have been planted it will not be necessary to feed them again until they have germinated. Only *water* will have to be applied.

After the seedlings have appeared, feed weekly with dry powder. Apply it as thinly as possible down the rows and water in. Avoid getting the dry powder on the foliage as this will scorch the leaves. As the plants grow, continue the periodic application of the dry powder. Eventually experience will guide the grower as to the frequency and amount of feed to apply. Liquid feed can also be used on a regular basis.

Such systems are so simple and differ so little from normal soil culture that it is difficult to use the term 'hydroponics'.

A variation of this method is where materials of high capillarity such as vermiculite or lignite are used, when drainage holes may be 2–3 in from the base in the side of the trench to allow a 'basement' supply of moisture and nutrients which is drawn to the surface by both the material itself and the growing plant. Should any problems arise, the aggregate can be flushed out with clean water. In the UK excellent crops of tomatoes, chrysanthemums and other crops have been grown under glass with the very minimum of attention. It is of some note that where seaweed-based Maxicrop has been used there has been considerable success, as this is a material which not only contains a whole range of trace elements but seems to have an inbuilt 'buffer' that avoids chemical imbalance.

In all cases use dry or liquid feeds on an almost constant basis, depending on the rate of growth exhibited and the ripeness of the plants themselves. *Do not hesitate to flood out with plain water and start again from scratch if plants show any unusual symptoms.*

CHAPTER SIX

Raising seedlings in vermiculite and other materials

Nothing gives the gardener greater pleasure than the sight of a seed-tray full of healthy seedlings. By the same token nothing is more disheartening than to find a mere six seedlings surviving from the sixty seeds originally planted. Yet only too often is this the case.

Seeds face many natural hazards before and during germination. After germination the seedling has many problems to overcome, such as disease, malnutrition, too much or too little water, insect pests, wind, and many other inclement factors.

To understand more about the germination process it is instructive to examine a seed in greater detail. Except in the case of orchids, most seeds are large enough for one to recognise that they are surrounded by a protective coat (testa) which can be removed easily from a soaked seed such as a pea. Within this coat lies the plant embryo consisting of a juvenile shoot (plumule) and a young root (radicle) with prominent seed leaves (cotyledons). Often these cotyledons are much enlarged and serve as storage tissue for the seed, but in many instances there is a specialised storage tissue (endosperm) quite distinct from the embryo. The essential features of the seed are the embryo and its associated food reserves.

When a seed is placed in moist soil, there is a rapid uptake of water. A small lettuce seed can take up enough water in 12 hr to increase its moisture content from 6 per cent to 75 per cent, but a larger seed such as a pea may take 2 days to achieve the same eventual water content. The uptake of water is slower at lower temperatures. The water taken up releases the embryo from its quiescent state, so that it grows large enough to rupture the testa. At the same time the food reserves break down so that the embryo will have sufficient nutrients to sustain it until it develops a root system to anchor it in the soil and absorb water and nutrients, and a shoot system with green leaves that can photosynthesise. The seed leaves can stay within the seed coat and below ground, as in the pea, but often they come above ground, turn green, and are the first organs to make use of light. In the dicotyledons there are two seed leaves, and in the monocotyledons one.

Vermiculite is an excellent medium for the hydroponic germination and raising of seedlings. But it is important that it should be fresh.

Some seeds prefer a pH of 4–5, which is well on the acid side. This can easily be arranged in the hydroponic method by adding sulphuric acid to the nutrient solution until the desired pH is reached (see p 91).

For many years now one of the authors (Dudley Harris) has used the method to be described and can highly recommend it for the ease with which clean, healthy, first-class seedlings are produced. In practice it differs very little from conventional seed-raising in soil.

In brief, a suitably shaped *container* or seed-tray with drainage holes is filled with vermiculite into which the *seeds are planted*. The vermiculite is watered periodically with a *nutrient solution* until the seedlings are ready for transplanting.

In the UK ground lignite has given excellent results as a seed-germinating medium, and worldwide research has involved materials as diverse as peat, wood bark, and a whole range of plastics, of which urea formaldehyde foam materials with their absorbency are more promising than 'closed cell' materials such as polystyrene foam.

THE SEED-TRAY

The seed-tray may be of any shape or size, but, generally, a

71

rectangular shape the length and width of a fruit or fish box and about 4 in deep is most suitable.

Plastic materials such as expanded polystyrene, polyvinyl-chloride (pvc) or polyethylene (polythene) are also used.

Polystyrene is excellent for seed-trays. It is a bad conductor, with the result that the vermiculite contained in seed-trays of this material is always 'warmer' than it would be in containers of better conducting materials. This is an obvious advantage for germinating seeds. A test may be made by placing one hand on expanded polystyrene and the other on asbestos-cement, standing side by side, under identical temperature conditions. The difference is astonishing.

With plastic materials no bitumen painting is necessary, unless a transparent or translucent plastic is chosen. It is, however, still necessary to stick a square of nylon filter over the holes in the bottom. A polyvinylacetate (pva) cement, sold under various brand names, is a good adhesive to use for this purpose.

Asbestos-cement seed trays have been manufactured and sold for many years. These are robust, work very well, and last practically indefinitely. They are available in three sizes and two depths, namely 3 and 5 in. The 3 in depth is the more suitable. Asbestos-cement seed-trays must be bituminised.

The ordinary fruit or fish box, though somewhat shallow, makes an effective and cheap seed-tray. Line it with a double-layer of kraft (bituminised) paper, which is obtainable from stationers. Punch a few holes in the paper for drainage purposes. Place as shallow a layer of drainage stones as possible and fill with vermiculite. A good kraft paper will last for one, possibly two, plantings.

Plasticised fibreboard trays have recently been introduced.

Paraffin cans cut in half may also be used if they are heavily painted with bitumen.

PREPARATION

The preparation of seed-trays and sowing of seeds follow exactly the directions given in Chapter Four for 'The Preparation

Steps in the preparation of a seed-tray

6 *Step 1 : Place a 1 in layer of drainage stones over the base*

7 *Step 2 : Pour in horticultural vermiculite to within ½ in of the top*

8 *Step 3 : Apply water with a fine rose*

9 *Step* 4 : *Draw parallel trenches in the moist vermiculite*

of Window-Boxes' from Step 1 to Step 9 (see p 50, and plates 6–9)· Omit the bitumen painting of plastic materials.

Buy only fresh seeds sold by reputable dealers. So many cases of failure can be traced to the use of old or infertile seed that to try to economise in this manner is foolhardy!

The seeds of the main families of soft plants can germinate almost after gathering, providing climatic conditions are correct, but the hard-wooded plants generally require a period of time before becoming capable of germinating.

Before planting, it is often helpful to soak very hard seeds in water overnight to help soften the outer coat.

FEEDING

Water the vermiculite or other material periodically with plain water or half-strength nutrient solution until the seedlings germinate. Avoid over-watering as this can cause fungal diseases, of which 'damping off' is only too familiar to the gardener. Try to water only sufficiently to produce that 'wetted and wrung out sponge' stage of moisture content.

According to the manufacturer's instructions (if you are using a commercial hydroponic nutrient powder), gradually increase the strength of the nutrient to full strength, about 10 days after germination. Again no hard-and-fast rules can be given. Some seeds germinate and grow faster than others. For instance, stock seeds can germinate $2\frac{1}{2}$ days after sowing during a warm sunny spring. The same seeds sown at the same time of the year during cold weather conditions could take up to 14 days to germinate.

A watering can, fitted with a fine rose, is recommended for applying nutrient solution.

Never allow seed-beds to dry out completely; nor should they be subjected to temperature extremes.

Out of doors ordinary light rain will do no harm to planted seed-trays or seedlings, although heavy rain may cause damage to the plants by seriously disturbing vermiculite around the delicate rootlets. In this case it would be advisable to provide temporary shelter.

Seedlings should be thinned out whenever necessary. This is usually done after they have grown about three leaves (excluding the seed leaves). Use a pricking-out stick carefully to separate an individual from the mass of seedlings. Place these into seed-trays prepared with vermiculite until they are ready to transplant into the hydroponic tank or into the garden.

Lack of light will always produce weak spindly seedlings. After germination bring on the seedlings in full sunlight unless they are shade-loving plants. The latter do require shadier conditions for germination and development.

In a spell of very cold weather it would be advantageous to move the trays indoors or to a warm place until germination commences, after which they should *immediately* be moved back to their permanent position in the sunlight.

A $\frac{1}{8}$ in wire-mesh screen on a wooden frame provides useful shade and shelter to newly germinated seedlings. In temperate zones it is usual to germinate seeds in a warm greenhouse, and more usual also to cover the seed-trays with paper for a few days until the seeds germinate, when the paper is removed.

TRANSPLANTING

The ultimate aim of the gardener is to transplant the seedling from the seed-tray into its final position in the garden, greenhouse or hydroponic tank. In this respect vermiculite has a distinct advantage over other media for the following reason: when the seedling is removed from the tray, a clump of vermiculite remains attached to the well developed root system, ensuring not only a 'built-in' moisture reservoir but also a readily available nutrient supply. The significance of this is the *minimum set-back and wilting of the transplant in its new surroundings*. Such an advantage hardly needs stressing. With other materials, such as peat or ground lignite, similar results prevail.

Seedlings are effectively removed from their trays without damage by using either the bowl of a teaspoon or small kitchen fork. It seems needless to add that the vermiculite or other material left clinging to the rootlet must not be shaken off.

The following summarises the advantages of the hydroponic method of seed-raising:

(1) A maximum percentage germination (strike) of seeds is obtained.
(2) Seedlings are always healthy, having been fed with correctly balanced nutrient solutions.
(3) The superior water-holding capacity of vermiculite ensures less chance of drying out — usually fatal to germinating seeds.
(4) After transplanting there is a minimum of danger from wilting and consequent shock.
(5) There is no need to prepare a special soil.
(6) A 'fresh' material such as vermiculite, lignite, plastics, and to a lesser extent peat, is sterile, hence a minimum of danger from soil-borne disease.
(7) There are no soil-borne weeds to worry about.

PART TWO

CHAPTER SEVEN

Commercial sub-irrigation in gravel

I. CONSTRUCTION AND OPERATION OF TANKS

The following notes apply mainly to large-scale crop production out of doors in suitable climates, it being doubtful whether it is economically feasible to consider large-scale soil irrigation systems out of doors in a temperate zone, because of the restricted usage during the winter months. Nevertheless it will be appreciated that there can be ready adaptability of the systems described for greenhouses of sufficiently large area.

Without any doubt, commercial hydroponics by gravel sub-irrigation is the most effective as well as the most popular method yet devised. It has every advantage and very few disadvantages.

Sub-irrigation in gravel is most suited to automation. Although the initial outlay of construction is higher than with other methods, the labour costs involved in an automatic system are minimal. Plant nutrient and water are used in the most economical manner possible.

Gravel sub-irrigation is the nearest approach to the 'assembly line' production of crops; the nutrient formula and medium remain constant, only the climate varies (and even this can be controlled to a large extent in a greenhouse).

THE DIRECT FEED SYSTEM

In this system, first suggested by Purdue University, a water-tight container about 4 ft wide, approximately 10 in deep and any reasonable length is constructed in concrete, or concrete and bricks. There is a central drainage channel with a perforated cover. Over this a 1 in layer of coarse stones, about $\frac{1}{2}$ or $\frac{3}{4}$ in in size, is placed, followed by $\frac{1}{8}$ in gravel chip to within $\frac{1}{2}$ in of the top. The nutrient solution is stored in a reservoir partially sunk in the ground. The nutrient is pumped through a pipe into the channel whence it seeps out through the gravel, gradually rising towards the surface. At a predetermined height the pump is switched off and the liquid allowed to gravitate back into the reservoir. Water is added to the nutrient solution in the reservoir to restore that lost by evaporation.

By using a time-clock in conjunction with the pump, together with a ball float-valve in the reservoir, the whole installation can be made automatic.

Let us consider the step-by-step construction of a typical gravel sub-irrigated tank. This particular tank is completely automatic. It is by no means the only method of construction, but well illustrates the first principles of the Direct Feed System of gravel sub-irrigation. Many large commercial installations are based on this same design.

Any 'backyard' gardening enthusiast, in a suitable climate to get year-round use, could build a hydroponic tank of this type himself. If necessary, outside labour may be hired to dig the excavations, mix the mortar and lay the concrete units.

The shape of the tank described is not rectangular, but has been constructed to conform with the contours of the garden.

Select and peg out a sunny site. The position should be as wind-protected as possible.

Excavate 6 in below the level of the surrounding ground and grade until the base is level and even. On sloping ground it will be necessary to build up the lower-lying areas.

Water the excavation thoroughly and compact it as much as possible. The correct preparation of the base ground is *vitally* important.

Allow at least 18 in for paths all around the proposed structure. Mark out with string a parallel strip exactly 24 in wide, and the length of the tank. A 50 ft length is convenient. One-half of the base of the tank, consisting of pavement slabs 24 in square × 2 in thick, will be built on this strip.

In the centre of the excavation, next to the first layer of slabs, rough-dig a trench the length of the tank. This is to accommodate the drainage channel and should be about 10 in wide and 8 in deep.

Place the paving slabs, with their edges parallel, side by side the length of the tank. These must be well bedded in at least 4 in of builder's sand. The slabs should be at the same level throughout and this must be carefully checked. Allow a small fall of at least $\frac{1}{2}$ in from outer to inner edge (see Fig 14). There is about $\frac{1}{2}$ in space between each slab. Fill this initially with sand. Compact the channel excavation, using plenty of water and small stones.

Place the drainage channel sections (4 ft 6 in long; 3 in radius; 10 in wide) next to the first layer of slabs interlocking one section with the next and allowing at least $\frac{1}{2}$ in between sides of slab and channel. The channel must also be bedded down in builder's sand.

Allow a 1 in fall from one end of the channel to the other (pump) end. This is very important and is readily contrived by placing the first section (farthest from the pump end) with its side exactly level with the edge of the slab. Each section should be placed a little lower until the edge of the last section is at least 1 in lower than the edges of the paving slabs next to it. Now place the other layer of slabs next to the channel.

Pour water into all joints to wash in the sand. Make a 3:1 sand/cement mortar with the addition of a waterproofing agent if desired. With the aid of a bricklayer's trowel fill all joints, tamping down as much as possible. It is very important to exercise great care in mortaring these joints otherwise movement cracks might subsequently appear. These can easily be repaired should they occur. *Placement of the slabs on a 1 in concrete base will ensure a more stable structure.*

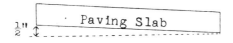

$\frac{1}{2}$"

Paving Slab

Fig 14 *Shows $\frac{1}{2}$-in fall from outer to inner edge of slab*

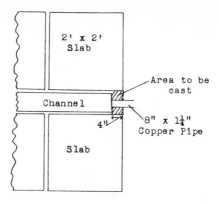

Fig 15 *Channel section cut off about* 4 *in short of end of last slab*

Into the pump end of the tank, a copper pipe 8 in long by $1\frac{1}{4}$ in internal diameter (i.d.) must be cast. This is both the entrance and drainage pipe for the nutrient solution.

Make provision for this pipe by cutting the last section of the drainage channel 4 in short of the end of the last slab (Fig 15).

Support the pipe in position with the aid of box-wood shuttering cut with a hole in it to accommodate the pipe. The latter must be quite level and its bottom internal surface must be flush with the lowest point in the drainage channel. Use a 4:3:1 concrete with a $\frac{1}{8}$ or $\frac{1}{4}$ in aggregate. At least 4 in of pipe will jut out from the end of the tank.

Using red hard bricks on edge, build a single layer around the periphery of the entire slab. Employ a 3:1 mortar for all bondings. Build a second layer on top of the first. The depth from the top of the bricks to the base will be about 10 in. This depth is sufficient for most purposes. The tank at this stage, consisting of slab, channel and bricks, is shown in plate 10.

Plaster the internal brick surfaces with a 3:1 mortar and finish the top of the bricks with a $\frac{3}{4}$ in coping.

After allowing one week to dry, paint the entire internal surfaces with a bitumen *emulsion*. The idea of using an emulsion at this stage is to obtain a better bonding with the mortar which might still retain more or less moisture.

10 *Completed tank consisting of base, channel and brick wall*

Twenty-four hours later, or when completely dry, apply a second coat using a bitumen *solution*. Include the coping in the second treatment.

Prepare a drainage cover, which can be made by cutting strips of asbestos-cement. This can be purchased in sheets 4 ft wide, 8 ft long and $\frac{3}{16}$ in thick. Cut into 4 ft long strips at least 9 in wide (see plate 11).

Drill three rows of $\frac{1}{8}$ in holes running the length of each strip, and, after painting twice with the bitumen solution, place the strips end to end over the drainage channel. Make sure the drilled holes are not blocked with bitumen.

Place a $1\frac{1}{2}$ in layer of $\frac{1}{2}$ in to $\frac{3}{4}$ in aggregate (small stones) over the drainage channel covering a width of about 18 in (see plate 12).

Over the entire base place $\frac{1}{8}$ in gravel chip to within $\frac{1}{4}$ in of the top of the coping. The gravel used in Dudley Harris's tank is Malmesbury blue-stone – a metamorphosed shale. Any suitable gravel, as long as it is inert (does not contain undesirable materials, such as limestone), may be used. It is advisable, though

81

11 *Place a cover over the channel*

not essential, to wash out the fines (silt etc) which some gravels contain, before placing in the tank.

The completed tank, filled with gravel, is illustrated in plate 13.

To connect the tank, place in the end of the copper pipe a rubber bung drilled with a 1 in hole to receive a pvc $\frac{3}{4}$ in id straight adaptor. Screw this into a 1 in gatevalve. Use 1 in id pvc for all piping. Pvc elbows, T-pieces, straight adaptors of $\frac{3}{4}$ in id and 1 in outer diameter (od) are easily procurable. (See also Fig 16.) Screw-type hose clips are used where necessary.

Connect the tube leading from the copper pipe via the gate-valve (1) with the discharge port of a small centrifugal pump. A 'Stuart-Turner' Model No 12 is shown (plate 14 and Fig 16). The intake port runs into the nutrient reservoir – a 300 gallon asbestos-cement barrel-type tank in this case. A threaded pvc elbow and straight adaptor connects a pvc tubing to a foot-valve at the bottom of the reservoir. The threaded pvc elbow is held in place by rigid pvc threaded pipe running through the wall of the

12 Place a 1½in thick layer of coarse aggregate around the drainage cover

13 Completed tank with gravel

14 Connect with pvc piping to pump and reservoir

reservoir and sealed with rubber washers – one on each side of the reservoir wall. A galvanised backing nut holds the rigid pvc in place.

The position of the pump is arranged so that the level of the nutrient solution, after topping up with water, is always above the pump. In this way the pump is always primed. A by-pass connexion with gatevalve is connected on the discharge side of the pump. This valve (2), leading into the rigid pvc tube, can be seen in the photograph. A waste pipe and valve (3) are also useful in the system. These may be placed between the by-pass connexion and valve (1).

The pump, which is mounted on a small concrete slab, is connected to the electric mains, via a time-clock if desired. It is protected with a weatherproof box and lid.

Fig 16 will help to clarify the relationship of tank to pump, pipe-lines, reservoirs, and gatevalves.

Fig 17 shows transverse relationship of reservoir, pump and tank.

Paint the asbestos-cement barrel-reservoir inside with two coats of bitumen solution and allow to dry thoroughly. The top of this reservoir must be at least 1 ft below the base of the tank. More often than not it has to be sunk in the ground. A lid for the

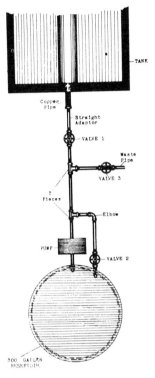

Fig 16 *Plan of tank, reservoir, pump, pipe-lines, and valves*

reservoir is essential.

In the automatic system a cistern-type ball float-valve connected to the water mains is affixed as near as possible to the top of the reservoir. With manual operation this may be omitted altogether.

The above description is bound to bring forth many questions:

'Can I use brass or galvanised fittings instead of plastic?'

'What about a staking system?'

'Is it satisfactory to use ordinary paint?' etc.

Many of these questions will be adequately dealt with in the next chapter.

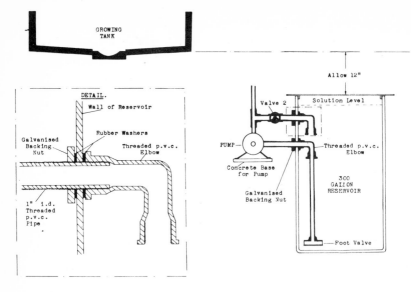

Fig 17 *Relationship of tank to reservoir and pump in transverse section*

QUANTITIES, MATERIALS, COST

It was mentioned above that the initial outlay of constructing a concrete sub-irrigated tank is higher than for the other methods of hydroponic growing. But costs are always relative. While bearing in mind the facts that the concrete or concrete and brick sub-irrigated tank is permanent, requires little or no maintenance and, if automatic, cuts down tremendously on labour expenses (more often than not the greatest expense), then this initial outlay is well spent.

A very important point to consider here is that ten hydroponic tank units of the same type could be operated by one *larger* pump and with one *larger* reservoir. This would reduce the unit cost considerably. The largest items of expense are the pump and reservoir.

Instead of the small pump of the type described, which is capable of delivering 600 gallons an hour at a 5 ft head, a much larger pump capable of 5,000–6,000 gallons an hour could be used. By means of a manifold it would be an easy matter to subirrigate ten hydroponic tanks at the same time.

For $\frac{1}{8}$ in gravel, reckon on a reservoir capacity of at least 2 *gallons per sq ft of growing area of 9 in depth*. Ten tank units of 125 sq ft each would therefore require a reservoir capacity of at least 2,500 gallons.

MANUAL OPERATION

Manual operation of the tank is very simple. The grower has only to switch on the pump, adjust a few valves, and top up the reservoir with water at least once daily during the summer months, less during the winter months.

Referring to Fig 16, use the following procedure:

Step 1 – Open valve 1, shut valves 2 and 3.

Step 2 – Turn on pump. Nutrient solution will be forced into the channel and through the gravel particles. Allow the pump to operate until the level of the liquid reaches about 1 in from top of the gravel surface. This usually takes about 30 min.

Step 3 – Turn off pump.

Step 4 – Open valve 2, allowing the nutrient to drain back into the reservoir by gravity. This usually takes about three times as long as the pumping time.

Step 5 – From the water mains make up that volume of water lost by evaporation
(*a*) from the surface of the gravel, and
(*b*) by transpiration from the foliage of the plants.
This may be done at any convenient time between pumpings. In cool weather it may only be necessary to top up every second or third day. It is essential though to ensure that for the next pumping there is always sufficient water to fill the hydroponic tank completely, otherwise the pump is likely to run dry with disastrous consequences (to the pump!).

The five steps just mentioned are all that are basically

required to ensure that the plants receive their necessary water and nutrient elements.

AUTOMATIC SYSTEM

If you are one whose every moment of spare time is precious or irregular, the automatic system of sub-irrigation by time-clock and float-valve is a particular boon. This will afford the pleasures of hydroponic growing with a minimum of time spent on irrigation. Naturally the hardworking family man will be only too happy to devote an hour or so during the week-end to the tank, spraying, staking, picking and admiring.

For little extra cost a completely automatic tank may be fitted up. Only two extra items are required, namely:

(1) a time-clock and
(2) copper piping with appropriate fittings and a lavatory cistern type of ball float-valve.

This extra investment is well worth while.

The time-clock is placed in the circuit as shown in Fig 18.

The time-clock has 'on-off' tabs set on its dial. Suppose 30 min has been found by experiment to be the optimum pumping period. The 'on' tab is put at the time of day when pumping is to commence (in Dudley Harris's tank this is set for 11 am); while

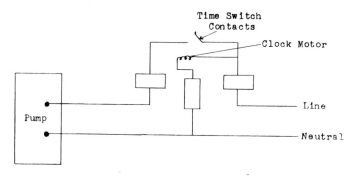

Fig 18 *Line diagram for 'Venner' time-clock*

the 'off' tab is set 30 min later. The clock mechanism will see to it that the pump is turned on daily at the time selected and off again after the half-hour period – or whatever other period may be chosen.

It is also possible to turn the pump on and off manually at the time-clock, quite independently and without upsetting the timing mechanism. This is most useful for adjusting pH of solutions or mixing a fresh batch of nutrient.

The time-clock may also be fitted with extra sets of 'on-off' tabs allowing two or three automatic pumping periods each 24 hr. The 'on-off' time period will become largely a matter of individual experiment and will depend on pump capacity, type of gravel, climatic conditions, and so on. For a 30 ft tank, with the type of pump mentioned above, the automatic pumping cycle should last between 30 and 40 min.

The ball float-valve is a comparatively inexpensive, but nevertheless indispensable, item to complete the automation of the hydroponic installation.

It will be necessary to purchase sufficient $\frac{1}{2}$ in copper piping to reach the reservoir from the nearest water-mains pipe. Do not forget to include all necessary T-joints, elbows, etc. A tap-valve will also be required to control the rate of drip through the ball float-valve.

To accommodate the ball float-valve, bore a hole near the top of the reservoir at such a height that when the valve is completely closed the reservoir is filled with the nutrient solution to its working level. Connect the outside of the ball float-valve to the tap-valve and then through to the existing water-supply mains via the copper tubing.

The automatic irrigation of the tank and topping up of reservoir has now been completely set up.

In addition to leaving valve 1 open, as in the manual system, valve 2 will have to be left open as well so that, at the end of the pumping cycle, the nutrient solution may flow back into the reservoir. With both valves 1 and 2 open, partial circulation of the nutrient through valve 2 will take place during pumping. Far from being a disadvantage, this extra circulation may be distinctly beneficial, although it will take a little longer to pump the solution to the correct height.

From the moment the level of the liquid in the reservoir begins to drop, the ball float-valve will start the water flow. This flow has to be adjusted from the tap at a drip rate so as to restore the nutrient solution in the reservoir to its working level.

On a hot day a tank filled with leafy plants can cause a water loss amounting to up to 10 per cent of the volume of the reservoir. This is about 30 gallons on a 300 gallon reservoir. Therefore a drip flow of about 30 gallons in, say 20 hr or approximately $1\frac{1}{2}$ gallons an hour must be arranged for. If the water is allowed to drip in at too fast a rate, then after the flow back of solution from the hydroponic tank, the extra water would cause overflowing and loss of nutrient.

On the other hand, in wet weather it may be necessary at times to turn off the mains water supply altogether. The manipulation of the water drip-feed, therefore, becomes a matter of experience. In dry weather it is a very simple matter to adjust this flow rate.

The hydroponic grower will soon find the particular conditions to suit his own installation and at this point the magic word 'automatic' begins to have some meaning. Weeks will go by with no adjustment to valves.

There are other devices for controlling the pumping and return of liquid to the reservoir. These are briefly listed as follows:

(1) Float switch in the hydroponic tank.
(2) Overflow pipe in the hydroponic tank activating trip-switch.
(3) Use of solenoid gate-valves with time-clock.
(4) Automatic siphon tubes.

The plant food

The remarks made in Chapter Four apply here, too. The grower has either the choice of making up his own formula (see Chapter Nine) or of using one of the commercially available 'complete' hydroponic nutrient powders.

Adjusting the pH

Dissolved in normal municipal waters at the rate of 1 lb per 50 gallons, most powders will give a solution pH value close to 6·0, the desired level for a vast majority of plants. A week or two after making up a fresh solution, and this applies particularly to newly constructed tanks, the pH value will tend to drift towards the alkaline side of the scale, ie above 7·0. It must be restored to 6·0 by the gradual addition of 50 per cent sulphuric acid. Employ the following procedure:

(1) Close valves 1 and 3, open valve 2.
(2) Turn pump on. This will cause the nutrient to circulate in the reservoir via the pump and by-pass pipe.
(3) Withdraw about 10 ml of liquid in a 6 in × $\frac{5}{8}$ in test-tube.
(4) Add 10 drops of a *Universal indicator solution*. (This is a special mixture of chemical indicator dyes which indicates a pH value by changing to a definite colour. The BDH Universal Indicator with a printed colour chart on the bottle is ideal for this purpose.) Observe the colour. Read off the pH value from the chart.
(5) If the pH value is above 6·0, make a small addition of 50 per cent sulphuric acid to the circulating liquid, repeating steps 3 and 4 until the correct pH has been reached.

As a *very rough guide* two thimblesful of 50 per cent sulphuric acid will reduce the pH of 300 gallons of a nutrient made up in most normal municipal waters from 6·5 to 6·0. Other waters could require considerably more acid for adjustment (see also p 112).

If, perchance, too much acid has been added, necessitating the addition of alkali, then use a slurry of builder's lime in exactly the same manner as described.

The determination and alteration of pH is really a very simple and speedy procedure. The hydroponic grower need have no fears about this at all.

NO OTHER CHEMICAL CONTROL IS NECESSARY

Mixing the plant food

Keeping valves 1 and 3 closed and valve 2 open, switch on the pump, whether it is being manually or automatically controlled. It is assumed that the reservoir has been filled with plain water to its working level, about 270 gallons for a 300–gallon asbestos-cement reservoir.

Slowly pour the nutrient powder into the circulating liquid. Allow the pump to run for 30 min. In order to allow all the plant food to be completely leached out by the water, leave the liquid standing overnight before use.

270 gallons of water at the rate of 1 lb each 50 gallons will require $5\frac{1}{2}$ lb of nutrient powder. This solution may be used over and over again for at least 4 weeks. The life of a fresh batch of plant nutrient solution will depend on several factors, among which may be mentioned the type of plant being grown, the stage of growth, the climatic conditions, and the concentration of plants per unit growing area. All these will affect the balance of the nutrient solution.

In the particular system just discussed the aim is to use a fresh batch of solution for as long a period as possible. When experience indicates that a depletion of one or more elements has taken place, the old batch is pumped away and replaced by a fresh one. In this manner the plants are assured of reasonably balanced solutions during their entire growing period.

AS A GENERAL GUIDE USE 1 LB OF NUTRIENT POWDER PER WEEK PER 100 SQ FT OF GROWING AREA. THIS APPLIES TO RAPID GROWING CONDITIONS – AND IS ONLY A GENERAL GUIDE. A LITTLE EXPERIENCE GOES A LONG WAY IN THIS MATTER.

To replace the old nutrient solution with a fresh one, pump the former away by closing valves 1 and 2 and opening valve 3. Fill the reservoir with fresh water and make up a new mixture.

An alternative method of operation requires analysis of the nutrient solution and addition of the necessary replacement chemicals. This system can only be profitably operated by very large installations. The cost of using a commercial powder or even of making up a formulation for use by the batch method is, in the long run, as low as the chemical replacement method.

Running costs, profit and loss

The costs of running hydroponic systems are reasonably low and involve adding the cost of water (either charged at a flat rate or a value to the costs of nutrients). For a 30 ft × 4 ft installation – if the norm of 1 lb of plant food per week is taken, plus 140 gallons of water – a fairly accurate figure is forthcoming. To this must be added the cost of depreciation at the rate of 10 per cent per annum and labour costs, which will in a commercial situation be charged in any case. It is outside the scope of this book to give detailed crop costings, but running costs are highly competitive with conventional soil culture, coupled with a very high level of crop productivity. However, the reader must be realistic about the costs of installing hydroponic equipment for low value crops, and it is not the purpose of this book to encourage anyone to do so, unless special circumstances prevail.

IMPORTANT NOTE

The following notes apply to culture under South African conditions out of doors, but because of their relevance in parts of America, Australia and other countries they have not been omitted. Readers in the temperate zones must note, however, that they do not apply to outdoor conditions in the United Kingdom, although they obviously have relevance under glass as they show the extreme diversity of cropping with hydroponics.

Crops

Since Chapter Ten will be devoted to the hydroponic culture of specific crops, only brief mention will be made here.

Virtually anything which can be grown in soil may be grown in the gravel tanks described above. Of course certain crops are more adaptable to hydroponic conditions than others. Even small seeds such as petunia or carrot may be directly sown in gravel. Special care must be taken to see that the gravel does not dry out during the germination period. One means of doing this is to cover the area sown with a fine gauze, which helps to keep it cool and hence moist. It may even be necessary during the warm part of the day to give a sprinkling of water in addition to the daily irrigation, especially under glass. As soon as germination has commenced, the young seedling will gradually fend for itself.

Dudley Harris has grown the following plants at one time or another in gravel: anemone, angelica, antirrhinum, beetroot, bean, chincherinchee, carrot, celery, chrysanthemum, carnation, chili, cucumber, cineraria, daffodil, delphinium, dahlia, freesia, fritonia, gladiolus, lettuce, nerine, nemesia, onion, mint, maize, petunia, pea, parsley, pepper (green), potato, radish, ranunculus, rose, strawberry, tomato, zinnia.

Plates 15 and 16 serve to illustrate the time sequence and rate of growth of plants planted into the gravel tank described.

The first, plate 15, shows pompon dahlias, 210 gladioli in 6 rows, zinnias, dahlias planted from seed, and tomatoes, put into gravel, 29 September–13 October 1963. Photograph taken on 20 October. It is possible to plant about 3,000 1 in gladioli corms in the entire tank area.

The second, plate 16, shows the same crops on 23 November 1963. The tomatoes were damaged by a succession of heavy winds and replaced, in some cases, twice. Lettuces are noticeable at far end of tank, transplanted 21 October 1963.

Plate 17 shows lettuce in gravel. They are crisp and have a delicious flavour. They take about 8 weeks from seedling to maturity in summer.

Advantages of Gravel Sub-irrigation

1. *Constant replenishment of air supply.* Providing a gravel of the correct size is used as a medium, the sub-irrigation method ensures at least a daily change of root atmosphere. When the fresh liquid is pumped into the gravel, it displaces the old air; on drainage back into the reservoir, fresh air is sucked into the gravel. The

15 *Pompon dahlias, gladioli, zinnias, tomatoes. Photograph taken on* 20 *October* 1963

16 *The same plants a month later*

17 *Crisp firm lettuce heads*

18 *Profusion of pompon dahlias*

vital function of air was discussed in the first chapter.

It is interesting to note that one can actually hear the fresh air being sucked into the gravel as the nutrient solution returns to the reservoir. This sound may be approximately imitated by touching the palate with the tip of the tongue and gently sucking air through the mouth.

A further beneficial supplementary effect is probably derived by partial circulation of the nutrient solution through valve 2 during pumping.

2. *Ease of automation.* The sub-irrigation system in gravel lends itself most easily to automatic devices, leading to lower labour costs. This is a distinct advantage.

3. *Economy of plant nutrients.* Sub-irrigation allows plant nutrient solutions to be used for the longest period. At the same time this method affords the easiest means of control of pH and chemical elements.

4. *Ease of sterilisation and extermination of certain pests.* With sub-irrigation, the medium may be sterilised at suitable intervals with the greatest of ease, using formaldehyde. Cutworms, those destructive garden pests, are eliminated in rather a novel way. Pump the ordinary nutrient to the surface of the gravel and leave standing for about an hour. Result: all cutworms either drown or move to the surface of the liquid, where they can be removed and

destroyed.

The deliberate coupling of the terms 'gravel' and 'sub-irrigation' should be noted. Sand should not be sub-irrigated. Particularly with fine sands, because of the tendency for moisture to be held by capillarity in the voids, aeration may become a serious problem. Vermiculite should never be sub-irrigated.

Disadvantages of Gravel Sub-irrigation

1. *Relatively high costs of construction.* Gravel sub-irrigation requires the construction of waterproof beds and reservoirs. This usually involves concrete, which together with the cost of pumps, pipes, valves, time-clocks, makes for relatively high initial costs.

However, these costs are to a large extent offset by the saving of labour offered by the electrical devices. Furthermore the tanks constructed in concrete are durable and permanent.

2. *Looser anchorage than soil or sand.* This is rather a serious disadvantage but may largely be overcome by efficient staking systems.

Gravel refers to a particle size between $\frac{1}{16}$ and $\frac{3}{8}$ in. An ideal size for growing plants is $\frac{1}{16}$ to $\frac{1}{8}$ in. It may readily be imagined therefore that particles of this size cannot pack to the same extent as those of a loamy soil, for example. The result is a loose medium.

Tall plants, such as gladioli, with relatively shallow root systems, top heavy with large flowers, are apt to be blown about rather easily by the wind out of doors (see plate 16). This may be countered

(*a*) by building windbreaks, and/or
(*b*) by building a system of support for the plants either individually or in rows.

3. *Gravel suffers from temperature extremes.* Owing to its relatively high thermal conductivity, gravel is either too hot or too cold.

In the midsummer sun at the height of the day it is sometimes uncomfortable to place one's hand for more than a few seconds on a dark coloured gravel. On the other hand, gravel presents a chilling atmosphere for roots during cold nights. These extremes of temperature are not ideal for growing plants.

This description, although rather exaggerated, is nevertheless generally true. By placing an inch layer of $\frac{1}{2}$ in diameter stones of light colour, such as fresh granite, on top of the gravel surface the objection of overheating may largely be overcome. Artificial shading is another device which may be used for the same purpose.

Although not serious, the chilling effect is more difficult to deal with. Mixing gravel with peat moss or vermiculite is not practicable. It is possible, though expensive, to allow for the thermostatic heating of gravel.

It must be borne in mind that the heating effect applies more particularly to a *dark* stone which tends to absorb heat.

Other methods of construction of the Purdue Tank

The one advantage of constructing the hydroponic tank from pre-cast concrete units and bricks is simplicity and ease. This design is ideal for the not-too-handy person and avoids the extra expense of employing labour for making shuttering, casting concrete slabs and so on. At the same time it is a relatively cheap standard design made from readily obtainable units.

A disadvantage from which this design suffers, however, is the tendency for fine cracks to form between mortared bondings. In a 30 ft tank there are 28 bonds between the slabs, 2 longitudinal bonds between channel sections and slabs, and 6 bonds between channel units themselves.

If the tank is laid on clayey ground, movement cracks are likely to appear in the slab. In order to avoid subsequent repair work, it is best to apply a generous layer of a rubberised bitumen compound, such as 'Bostik' No 692 Sealer, over all the bonded areas at the time of construction of the slab.

Repairing the Slab

Should it become necessary to effect repairs on the slab, this work may only be undertaken after harvesting. The best procedure is to remove the gravel in sections corresponding with the channel covers.

First, carefully remove the fine gravel, distributing it either over other portions of the tank or on the ground nearby. When the coarse aggregate around the drainage channel is reached, place this to one side for subsequent drying out and screening to separate it from the admixed fine gravel. The channel covers can now be removed, thus laying bare a whole section of the slab.

After repairs have been carried out, and/or the channel unblocked if necessary, the aggregates are replaced.

Where adequate labour is available, complete tanks may be laid bare in a very short space of time.

It may also be found necessary after 3 or more years to remove the root residues from the gravel, which may show increasing signs of blockage. This can be effected by removing the gravel as just described and screening it through a sieve, thus separating most of the root residues from the growing medium.

The other methods of construction of the same type of tank are:

(a) casting the entire unit, including walls, in concrete, and,

(b) casting the slab or base only in concrete and building brick walls.

A. CASTING ENTIRE UNIT IN CONCRETE

The general design and outer dimensions can remain the same as the unitised structure described earlier in this chapter.

The thickness of the slab should be 3-4 in, with an extra 'bulge' in the middle to allow for the central channel. This should have a 5 in width and 3 in depth at the deepest (pump) end. The farthest end should be 2 in deep, allowing a 1 in fall in 50 ft.

Provide for a 3 in thickness of walls all round and a 9 in depth at the wall, sloping to a 10 in depth at the channel.

The structure may be built partly buried in the ground, but reinforcing of the base is an essential. For this purpose use six

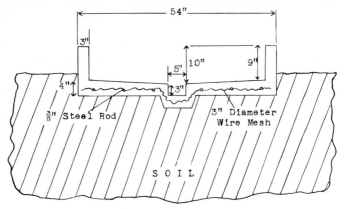

Fig 19 *Cross-section of an entirely concrete hydroponic tank*

$\frac{3}{8}$ in steel rods and 3 in diameter wire netting 4 ft wide. The base should be cast as level as possible.

It will be necessary to construct suitable shuttering to cast this structure but a unitised shuttering system can be designed for casting a number of tanks.

It is also possible to make up shuttering for casting the tank in sections. In this case bitumen must be melted into the joints and reinforcement is not necessary.

Fig 19 shows a diagrammatic cross-section of a typical tank cast entirely in concrete.

For casting use a 5 : 2½ : 1 concrete mixture, tamping down well.

A 4 ft 6 in × 30 ft concrete tank will need approximately the following quantities:

Cement	12 cwt.
Sand	2 cu yd
½ in stone	3 cu yd

B. SLAB CAST IN CONCRETE WITH BRICK WALLS

There seems little advantage in casting the slab only and building the wall in bricks, except that the construction of shuttering is somewhat simplified.

In this type of tank the slab is constructed to the same measurements and in exactly the same manner as the one described in A.

After the allowance of a week for the setting of the concrete, a two-course brick wall is built all round the periphery of the base, following instructions given on p 80.

Both types of tank are painted with bitumen, fitted with channel covers, connected to pump and reservoir, and filled with gravel.

Raised tanks

Tanks raised on concrete or brick piers are sometimes constructed, particularly where sloping ground is encountered. The raised tank has the distinct advantage of reducing bending for the grower, as well as discouraging the attentions of certain insect pests.

Since the shuttering for the concrete needs stays and props this slab is costlier to construct. Reinforcement of the slab is absolutely essential.

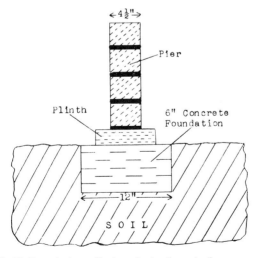

Fig 20 *Foundation, plinth and pier for raised concrete slab*

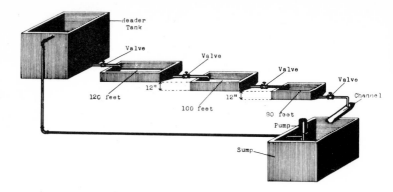

Fig 21 *The Gravity Feed System of hydroponics*

A 30 ft long tank would need six piers, 6 ft apart.

For the foundations, dig six trenches, 6 in deep, 12 in wide and about a foot longer than the width of the proposed tank. Fill each trench with 6 : 3 : 1 concrete mixture. When set, build a single course of bricks as a plinth for the pier. On this plinth build the $4\frac{1}{2}$ in thick pier to the desired height (Fig 20).

OTHER SYSTEMS OF GRAVEL SUB-IRRIGATION
1. GRAVITY FEED

This system utilises, as its name suggests, the principle of gravity filling.

Usually beds are arranged on sloping ground one below the other. Nutrient solution is stored in a header tank raised a few feet above the first bed. The flow of solution is controlled by a valve. Beds are constructed according to the design already described for sub-irrigation. The one essential difference is that, at the end of each bed, a valve is opened to allow liquid to flow to the next bed below it. Sometimes an automatic siphon device replaces the valve. Finally the nutrient solution flows into a sump from which it is pumped back into the header tank (Fig 21).

To compensate for the loss of liquid by evaporation and transpiration, each tank is 20 per cent less in length than the one preceding it.

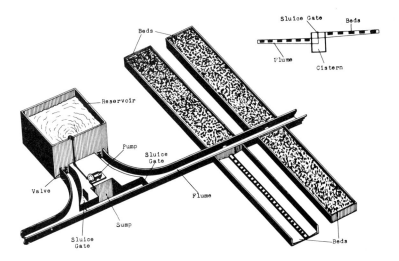

Fig 22 Gravel sub-irrigation with the flume system

In America a three-bed system of dimensions 120, 100, and 80 ft in length, and 4 ft wide, is popular.

The sump is the main storage reservoir for the system. Its total capacity need only be sufficient for the *first* bed, ie 2 gallons per sq ft of growing area for gravel.

From this brief description it will be readily realised that the gravity system affords a large saving in reservoir and pump capacity.

By means of a time-clock, solenoid valves, and float switches, the whole system can be made automatic.

2. FLUME SYSTEM

In this method of gravel sub-irrigation, a series of beds is built on *exactly the same level* parallel with one another.

At right-angles to the ends of the beds, a flume or channel at least 12 in deep and 12–18 in wide is constructed. The *flume* has a fall from its upper to lower end (next to sump or reservoir).

The nutrient solution, entering the flume via a valve from an above-ground reservoir, flows along it into each bed. When the liquid is at the correct height in the beds, and this is the reason the beds have to built at exactly the same level, a sluice gate is opened through which the liquid drains into a sump. From here it is pumped back into the reservoir. Water may be added if necessary and the duplicate section of beds on the other side similarly irrigated. (See Fig 22.)

The flume system saves tremendously in pump capacity. But the reservoir has to be large enough to fill at least one section of the beds at a time.

The construction of large flume systems is quite an undertaking.

CHAPTER EIGHT

Commercial sub-irrigation in gravel

II. TECHNICAL FACTORS AFFECTING GROWTH

Many questions bother the novice about to embark on his first hydroponic venture. Experience with the hydroponic method, trial and error or 'hit and miss' tactics will eventually provide many of the answers, but by this time the enthusiast may very well have lost much of his enthusiasm.

It is the object of this chapter, therefore, to provide the answers to such questions as:
What is pH value?
How do I determine pH value?
Is my water suitable?
How often must I irrigate?
To what level should I irrigate?
What do I do about rain out of doors?
Wind? and so on.

For convenience, the subject matter has been divided into

(A) Nutrient environment.
(B) Medium environment.
(C) Climatic environment.

A. NUTRIENT ENVIRONMENT

Without water life would be impossible on our earth. The converse of this statement—'with water life is possible'—is true, up to a point. If the word 'suitable' is inserted before the word 'water', we shall be much nearer the truth of the matter; for without a *suitable* type of water agriculture would not be possible.

105

Pure water is, strange as it may seem, an exceedingly rare substance confined almost exclusively to scientific laboratories. All water contains dissolved solids and gases which affect its quality and limit it for certain uses. For example, no one could exist for long on sea-water as his sole source of drinking-water. This is because sea-water has large amounts of dissolved solids—3·6 per cent on average. About 2·6 per cent of sea-water consists of common salt. This we can readily taste. Repeated ingestion of quantities of this water would soon affect our systems, leading eventually to sickness and death.

This same state of affairs exists with plants, only these are markedly less tolerant to the dissolved solids in water than are humans.

In other words, any system of agriculture, of which hydroponics is a type, is entirely limited by the quality of water which is available to the plants. Water can always be purified by one means or another to render it suitable, but at the present time this is a somewhat costly business and is not a practical answer to the problem.

Very generally speaking, a water which is suitable for drinking purposes may be used for hydroponics. Most municipal waters are entirely satisfactory for use.

Many municipalities and water boards will provide, on request, an analysis which can include the following:

> pH—a measure of alkalinity/acidity
> Conductivity—a measure of total dissolved salts
> Total solids
> Chloride ion (Cl^-)
> Sulphate ion (SO_4^{--})
> Calcium ion (Ca^{++})
> Magnesium ion (Mg^{++})
> Bicarbonate ion (HCO_3^-)
> Iron as ferrous ion (Fe^{++})
> Total hardness
> Temporary hardness

It is important to know where the sample was taken, since very soft waters are able to take into solution the metals of the pipes through which they run. If such a water has been in contact with iron pipes, the Fe^{++} level is raised, but this is not harmful. If it has flowed through a long run of lead or copper pipes, metallic ions of these metals can be present. Water from peaty watersheds will have high total solids and low conductivities, and the remarks below relating to total solids apply to waters from mineral watersheds.

'Hardness' in water is commonly due to the chlorides, sulphates and bicarbonates of calcium and magnesium. The term is derived from the fact that 'hard' waters produce a scum when soap is lathered in them.

'Hardness' in itself is no great problem when considering the water for agricultural purposes. The presence of sodium chloride is far more serious. A water with a chloride content exceeding 200 ppm as Cl should be regarded with suspicion.

It should be noted here that a make-up water with say a 100 ppm chloride content will tend to cause a build-up of chloride through daily additions in the sub-irrigation system. For example:

Initial chloride content of nutrient 20 ppm

Final chloride content of nutrient 62 ppm

This build-up results from adding a daily 10 per cent make-up of the nutrient reservoir by tap water with a chloride content of 20 ppm. If a greater make-up is necessary, as in warm summer weather, then the chloride level will rise faster.

There are other toxic substances sometimes found in water which are likely to spoil it for growing plants. These are the presence of certain toxic amounts of *metallic elements* such as zinc, copper and lead; also other non-metallic substances such as *sulphides* and *free chlorine*. The former is rather rare and not likely to be encountered, but the latter is more commonly found. Chlorine in the uncombined state is definitely toxic to plants. It injures the roots and, if present in high concentrations, produces a hardening of the plant. The amount normally present in drinking water is well below toxic limits, but occasionally toxic amounts are added during epidemics. Most of the free *chlorine* may be removed from water by letting it stand in the open air for several hours. This will not of course alter the *dissolved chloride* in the water. There is no way of reducing the chloride content of water other than by distillation or by electrical methods through semi-permeable membranes.

The hydroponic grower about to start a project is advised, therefore, to have his water analysed for

(1) total solids;
(2) chlorides (if [1] exceeds 500 ppm);
(3) total hardness (if high, then calcium and magnesium);
(4) pH value;
(5) heavy metals, sulphide, and 'free' chlorine only when suspected.

Most municipalities will supply suitable quality irrigation water, though when in doubt have this checked by analysis.

Many of the more remote parts of the world rely on boreholes and wells for their water supply. These should be analysed, especially if taste shows them to be brackish.

If sufficient can be collected, rain-water is an excellent source of supply.

What is pH value?

Whether dealing with conventional agriculture or hydroponics, 'pH' is an extremely important factor. When poorly controlled, or not controlled at all, plants either become sick or die. When the subject of hydroponics is discussed, it seems that even the most non-technical person has heard of pH. Unfortunately, the very term 'pH' value introduces an air of mystery, which scares many people. Actually the matter is a very simple one.

For the technically minded, the concept and symbol pH was introduced by a Swedish mathematician, Sorenson, in 1909, to denote the relative acidity (hydrogen ion concentration) of any solution. The quantity pH is the negative logarithm to the base

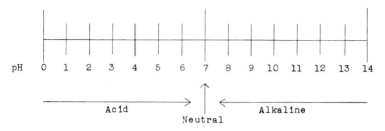

Fig 23 *The pH scale*

10 of the hydrogen ion concentration. The mode of expression has the advantage that all degrees of acidity or alkalinity are expressed by a series of positive numbers between 0 and 14. In plain words pH is merely a mathematically derived scale relating to the acidity or alkalinity of solutions. Pure water is neutral ,and is given the number in the middle of the scale, 7. Pure water has a pH value of 7·0. Those values between 0 and 7 are therefore degrees of acidity, whereas 7–14 denote degrees of alkalinity. The pH scale may roughly be compared with the keyboard scale of a piano. The middle of the piano would be like pH 7·0. The notes towards bass are analogous with the pH values 7–0; those towards treble with pH values 7–14.

It will be realised after reading the foregoing that a pH value of 5 denotes a concentration of hydrogen ion (acid) ten times greater than that of pH 6. A change of only one pH unit means a tenfold increase or decrease of acid concentration. Expecting a plant to grow well at a pH 5·0 when it prefers pH 6·0 is analogous to eating ten ice-creams when you should only eat one. You will probably become quite ill!

This is the reason why proper pH control is rather important for growing plants successfully. Each type of plant functions best within a definite pH range. Generally, most plants are at their best between pH 5·0 and 6·5, with 6·0 being an excellent happy medium. *This is therefore the recommended pH to aim for.*

Plant types do differ in their pH preference. There are the so-called 'acid-loving' plants (pH 4·0–5·0) such as the azalea, camellia, hydrangea, orchid and protea. There are the so-called

109

'lime-loving' plants (pH 7·0–8·0) such as sweet pea and stock.

A pH value of 4·0 is usually accepted as the lowest tolerated by plants in hydroponic culture. Root growth is retarded and even injured under such acid conditions. When plants are grown in a solution of pH below 5·0, rather high levels of calcium are required for satisfactory growth.

Similarly, alkaline solutions above 7·0 cause complications in the hydroponic method. The reason for this is that a high pH causes precipitation of iron, manganese, phosphorus, calcium and magnesium. Some or all of these become unavailable to the plant, causing deficiency symptoms and, if prolonged, death.

One of the difficulties the hydroponic grower comes up against is the maintenance of a sufficient level of iron in solution to satisfy the plant's needs.

Iron is usually supplied in the ferrous state as the sulphate. Under slightly alkaline conditions this becomes unavailable to the plant, after oxidation to the ferric condition. It is important, therefore, to keep the pH slightly on the acid side.

When the pH of the nutrient solution has been properly controlled, it will not be necessary to add extra iron, over and above that initially supplied in the trace elements. The reason for this is that, under slightly acid conditions, traces of iron become available to the plant from impurities in the gravel, or in the chemicals supplying the macro nutrients.

How to find the pH value

Many people are under the impression that there is something difficult or complicated about determining the pH value of a nutrient solution. Why this should be is rather strange, for the determination of pH, to a degree of accuracy suitable for hydroponic growing, is as easy, if not easier, than taking your temperature!

Three methods exist. These are:

(1) Indicator paper.
(2) Indicator solution.

110

(3)   Electric means.

(1)   *Indicator paper*
It is possible to obtain paper impregnated with indicator dyes. The pH values are denoted by the colour they change to when dipped in the solution. Such chemical supply houses as British Drug Houses, Merck, Johnson, La Motte, to name a few, manufacture these papers. There are also available 'wide-range' papers, which indicate pH values from say 4·0 to 8·0 in units of 0·5, as well as 'narrow-range' papers, such as chlorophenol red, which indicate a closer range, eg 5·2 to 6·8, in units of 0·2.

One can purchase indicator papers with two or three parallel strips of different colours. These are easier to read than the single colour papers.

Determining pH. Break off a $\frac{1}{2}$ in strip of the paper and dip it into the solution to be tested. After 20 sec remove and observe the colour. Compare this with the printed colour chart and read off the corresponding pH value.

Note that litmus paper is quite useless for indicating pH values in hydroponics.

The indicator papers, though simple and quick, are less accurate than the indicator solutions. This second method is therefore recommended for hydroponic growers.

(2)   *Indicator Solutions*
Indicator solutions may be purchased at most chemical supply houses. To find the pH of a solution, dip a 6 in by $\frac{5}{8}$ in test-tube in the nutrient solution to be tested and withdraw a 10 ml sample (about one-third of the test tube). Add 10 drops of the indicator solution. Note the colour after shaking, and read off the corresponding pH value from the printed colour chart on the bottle. The whole operation takes about 30 sec to perform.

It is best to have a Universal Indicator solution (the BDH solution indicates from pH 4·0 to 10·5 in units of 0·5) as well as some 'close-range' indicators. Eventually, with experience, the Universal Indicator alone will suffice.

For larger installations a colour comparator is useful. These employ coloured discs corresponding to the different pH values. By using two different indicator dyes (such as bromo-cresol purple and bromo-thymol blue) with the appropriate colour discs, it is possible accurately to read pH in units of 0·2 in the range 5·2 to 7·6.

The test-tube method, however, is accurate enough for most purposes, and the cost trifling.

(3) *Electrometric pH determination*

For extreme accuracy, rarely necessary in normal commercial practice, the *electric pH meter* is available. Most instruments have two electrodes, the hydrogen and reference electrodes, which when dipped in the solution will give the pH value to within 0·02 pH unit. Such models as Beckmann, Cambridge, Metrohm and Radiometer are well known in science laboratories.

Electrometric pH determination can only be recommended for large hydroponic installations, where many rapid pH determinations are required daily. Modern battery-operated portable models can be bought for £30 ($66).

How to alter pH (see also page 91)

Correction of Alkalinity. The uptake of nutrient elements by the plant usually leads to an alkaline drift in the solution. Put another way, the pH tends to rise to 7·0 and over. The alkalinity leached from cement or from a calcareous gravel also has the same effect.

To lower the pH, add 50 per cent sulphuric acid little by little while stirring or circulating the nutrient solution, until it has been restored to the desired level. This must be tested for by one or other method.

For small volumes of solutions (10 gallons) use a 10 per cent sulphuric acid. Larger volumes, up to 50 gallons, may be corrected with 25 per cent sulphuric, while up to 500 gallons or more would need 50 per cent acid. Large installations should use concentrated sulphuric acid. *Always bear in mind that this acid is extremely*

112

corrosive. Should it be spilt on your hands, flush generously with water immediately. Always add the acid to water, never water to acid.

The amount of acid necessary to restore the pH to 6·0 depends, among other things, on the buffering capacity of the water. Usually only a small quantity is necessary, but should the water have a high 'buffering' capacity as a result of a relatively high bicarbonate content, then larger quantities of acid will have to be used.

With small volumes, trial and error is the best way of finding out what quantity to use. Very soon experience will guide one.

The larger installations, using upwards of 10,000 gallons of water, can obtain the exact quantity of concentrated acid to bring any desired volume of water from any initial pH down to 6·0 by a simple laboratory titration. The following is the detailed procedure.

Place 500 ml of the water or nutrient solution to be tested in a 600 ml conical flask. Add about $1\frac{1}{2}$ ml of bromo-cresol purple indicator (0·1 per cent) (a purple colour is obtained if the pH is above 6·5). Now titrate with N/10 sulphuric acid in a burette until the colour changes to *yellowish with a suggestion of green* at pH 6·0. Note the burette reading in ml. This figure multiplied by 25 will give the number of ml of concentrated sulphuric acid to be added to 1,000 gallons of water or nutrient solution to bring the pH down to 6·0.

Correction of Acidity. The grower will not be called upon so often to correct an acid solution. However, should this become necessary, it is best done with a slurry of builder's lime as the source of alkali. Make this slurry in a bucket and by small additions bring the pH up to 6·0. Note that *limestone* (calcium carbonate), also loosely referred to in the trade as *lime*, is not suitable for correcting acidity. The procedure laid down in connection with acidifying with sulphuric acid applies here too. The one difference is that builder's (slaked) lime (calcium hydroxide) varies in composition from source to source. It is possible, though, by a similar titration method to work out the exact alkaline requirements of an acid solution.

The above remarks apply to solutions used for sub-irrigation methods. In other methods of feeding, the solution is not generally recovered for re-use.

Most commercial powders when dissolved at recommended strengths in municipal waters will give a pH value close to 6·0. Furthermore, if these are correctly formulated they should maintain this value for a reasonable period of time.

Water Acidification

One factor, often neglected, is the effect on pH of the constant addition of make-up water. Most municipal waters (tap) are, of necessity, alkaline. The waters of some authorities, for example, have an average pH value of 8·5, which means that every time this water is added to the reservoir, a certain amount of alkalinity goes with it. Fortunately, in this case, the buffering action is low, so that the effect is rather slight. Nevertheless it does have an effect. It is often simpler to adjust the make-up water to pH 6·0 *before* it is added to the main nutrient reservoir. On big installations it is common practice to do this in separate supply tanks. The adjusted water is then used to top up the nutrient.

How often should pH be checked?

This is a common question, and the answer depends on many factors. Experience is ultimately the only judge for establishing a set routine. It is recommended that pH be tested daily on large installations. For the small home tank, a test once or twice a week is sufficient. If experience indicates that the pH of a nutrient stays within the desired range for one or two weeks, then it will not have to be measured more frequently.

B. MEDIUM ENVIRONMENT

Earlier on, gravel was described as material belonging to a *size* group rather than conforming to a *type*. Aggregate between $\frac{1}{16}$ and $\frac{3}{8}$ in is recognized as gravel. Bigger material is 'stone', a smaller size becomes 'sand'.

Gravels differ enormously in size, porosity, shape, hardness and composition. All these factors, besides a few others, determine whether or not a gravel is suitable for hydroponics.

Primarily, a gravel that contains no toxic substances and provides good drainage and aeration will be suitable. Some of the factors governing these properties are now considered in greater detail.

(1) *Toxic substances must be absent.* Many media consist of cinders which may be acidic or alkaline. In this case they must be pretreated before use. Alkaline gravels are either soaked in a strong superphosphate solution or dilute sulphuric acid, while acidic substances may have to be leached with water or dilute alkali. Sulphurous compounds present in cinders could prove fatal to plant growth.

Most gravels contain fine dust or silt, and it is advisable to wash this out before placing in the hydroponic bed. A wet-screening through $\frac{1}{8}$ in mesh wire may be used to remove these fines.

On a relatively small scale, the fines may be largely removed by placing the gravel in a 4 gallon can and forcing through a strong jet of water. The fines tend to rise in the water and flow over the rim of the can. This is not a practicable method on a large scale, however.

(2) *Good moisture retention is essential.* Moisture retention is largely bound up with particle size. For certain given shapes a packing of smaller size particles produces smaller voids, hence greater capillary attractions, than larger size particles of the same substance. In other words, a rounded gravel of $\frac{1}{16}$ in diameter holds more moisture than a $\frac{3}{8}$ in rounded gravel of the same substance.

But *shape* is very important, too. Chippings, with their irregular facets, pack better and have a greater moisture-holding capacity than rounded particles of the same screen size.

The Malmesbury blue stone mentioned in Chapter Seven is a chipped $\frac{1}{8}$ in screened gravel. This has better water-holding properties than the $\frac{1}{8}$ in rounded gravel used in some of the beds at the CDM installation at Oranjemund.

The voids between the chips are smaller, hence more water is held within the medium by its stronger capillary attraction.

115

Porosity plays a part, too. Materials such as cinders and pumice hold moisture within the pores of the material. This allows the use of a gravel of larger size.

(3) *Good drainage is essential.* The key to success of the sub-irrigation system is good drainage, a fact already emphasised in Chapter Four. Its importance is so great that the word DRAINAGE should be impressed on anyone growing plants by the hydroponic method—in fact on anyone growing plants by any method.

Particle size is bound up with drainage and water retention. The presence of silt will adversely affect the drainage properties of gravel. All *free* liquid should be removed from the voids within the medium after gravitation back into the reservoir. The object is to leave a film of nutrient moisture around each gravel particle for nourishing the plant. The voids should be filled with air-saturated water vapour to allow normal respiration of root systems and healthy metabolic activity.

The beauty of the sub-irrigation system in gravel is the production in the medium of the environment just described. At the same time sub-irrigation generously provides root systems with a 'bonus', so to speak, in the form of fresh atmosphere daily.

It follows, therefore, that a compromise must be brought about between moisture retention on the one hand and good drainage on the other.

As time goes on, organic matter in the form of partly decomposed root, stem and leaf residues, as well as wind-blown soil and sand, tend to accumulate in the gravel. *Providing the drainage properties of the gravel have not been impaired,* this could be beneficial. Too great a quantity of extraneous silt or fine sand will inevitably lead to poor drainage. This condition must be watched carefully and can be remedied by washing out the fines as mentioned above.

(4) *Hardness.* Soft media, such as some cinders, are likely to break down with the production of fines. These tend to interfere with free drainage and should be avoided.

(5) *Sharpness.* Sharpness in a gravel can prove injurious, particularly to the crowns of plants. Young, soft plants such as

116

lettuce, may suffer irreparable damage through wind action out of doors. Sharp particles may cut the roots and stems of plants. Resulting injuries make it possible for disease-producing organisms to enter the plant tissues. Sharpness can be countered by using a 1 in blanket of larger stones of smoother form on top of the gravel.

The following is a partial list of different types of gravel suitable for sub-irrigation:

Granite
Shale
Sandstone
Brick (broken and screened)
Quartzite
Ironstone
Cinders (pretreated if necessary)
Pumice
Perlite
Lignite.

Irrigation Technique

The four most important pumping problems confronting the hydroponic grower in gravel are:

(1) how often to pump,
(2) when to pump,
(3) speed of pumping, and
(4) height to pump.

(1) *How often?*

The frequency of irrigation depends on several factors, such as the size and type of plants, the type of aggregate, and climatic conditions.

Leafy plants, such as lettuce, require more frequent irrigation than gladioli, for example. Smooth aggregates need more frequent irrigation than porous. Hot windy conditions tend to dry out

117

gravels, necessitating more frequent irrigation than cool wet conditions.

Generally speaking, in a warm climate *one irrigation a day in summer* is the rule. However, sometimes two or even three irrigations daily will be necessary.

Earlier in this chapter it was mentioned that the object of sub-irrigation was to leave a saturated, aerated atmosphere around the gravel particles. Although the nutrient chemicals dissolved in the film around the gravel particles will be steadily utilised by the plant, water will be absorbed at a much greater rate. As a result the nutrient film becomes more concentrated. Hence pumpings are arranged, firstly to satisfy the water requirements of the plant, and secondly the nutrient requirements. Assuming that replenishment of the nutrient chemicals did not take place, but all the necessary water was present, deficiency symptoms would show up within a few days. On the other hand, assuming that adequate nutrient was available to the plant, but not sufficient water, wilting would very soon occur. In other words, water, more than nutrient, is the limiting factor and the justification for more or less frequent irrigations.

(2) *When to pump?*

Once the daily irrigation routine has been established, the next question might well be 'What time of the day is best for pumping?'

For once-daily irrigations, the best time is during the warmest part of the day when the water needs of the plant are greatest. This would be between 11 am and 1 pm. For twice-daily pumpings, the morning and afternoon periods 8 am to 10 am and 2 pm to 3 pm respectively are recommended.

With automatic feeding by time-clock these periods present no difficulties. The manual operator, however, may be at his regular work during the day and cannot find opportunity to irrigate before, say, 5.30 pm. If possible, it is better to irrigate in the early morning before going to work. This is preferable to doing the process of irrigation at night.

118

(3) *How fast?*

This is a problem which is subject to much discussion. The speed of irrigation (and drain back) is very much connected with aeration of the root system. Too slow a pumping rate means a longer period of free-water in the void spaces, with a consequent lower oxygen supply. Too fast a pumping rate, however, can cause excessive turbulence and also lead to root damage through chafing. This fault may easily be remedied by the use of a by-pass pipe controlled by a valve and leading back into the reservoir. In any case it is an advantage to have such a pipe. By arranging a partial circulation of nutrient during pumping, complete air-saturation is ensured through air entrainment.

The usual recommendation is for a 30 min filling time, and a drainage period which lasts at least three times as long. The faster drainage takes place, though, the better. Faster drainage can be arranged by having a second pipe in the tank which can be opened after completion of pumping.

(4) *What height?*

The height of irrigation depends somewhat on the type of plant being grown. For young seedlings it is necessary to allow the nutrient to rise almost to the surface of the gravel. As soon as the plants grow, *aim to keep the top inch of the gravel dry*, thus preventing growth of algae. Certain fungal diseases are also discouraged by keeping a dry gravel surface. To aid in this respect it is important to have the beds filled evenly. Proper design will ensure this.

C. CLIMATIC ENVIRONMENT

The hydroponic grower, having mastered the techniques peculiar to this form of agriculture, is still faced with the tempestuous forces of Nature. A glorious crop of gladioli can be destroyed within minutes by a very short period of heavy wind. Growing under glass entirely overcomes this problem.

Since climatic factors are interacting, each must be considered in relation to the others.

119

(1) *Wind*

Wind is rather a troublesome problem. Its destructive effects are too well known.

One disadvantage of gravel culture is that the plant root system has a looser anchorage than it would have in a soil, owing to the greater compaction of the latter. The consequence of this is that even a fairly moderate wind will tend to blow over tall plants such as gladioli. Imagine the stately gladiolus with its long spike of mature blossoms. Its high centre of gravity causes tremendous leverage at the base when the wind blows. Without adequate support, gladioli are very easily blown about.

Another, less serious, consequence of wind is the increased rate of transpiration and evaporation leading to higher water losses. A very dry persistent wind will 'scorch' delicate plant tissue, such as that of lettuce and other susceptible plants.

What then is the remedy? Apart from the rather obvious course of building a greenhouse, it is imperative in areas of prevailing moderate or heavy winds to provide both windbreaks and an adequate staking system.

It is a well known principle that no attempt should be made to stop the wind altogether with a *solid* windbreak. Rather try to break it up into innocuous eddies by letting it blow *through* the barrier.

There are several types of materials used for this purpose. These include slatted wood, palm leaves, a line of willow trees, privet hedges, hessian cloth, and so on. The spacing between windbreaks and their angle, relative to the growing area, will depend on the size of the tanks, the wind velocity, and the presence of walls. Very often a neighbour's boundary wall acts as a reflector and it is possible for a damaging funnel of wind to blow apparently in the direction opposite to that prevailing.

Windbreaks should be constructed high enough to produce a protected area of sufficient width. It is generally reckoned that a given height affords protection for an area whose width is 4–5 times the height. Bear in mind, too, that the windbreak must not cut out any essential sunlight.

19 *Old boiler tube as support for a staking system*

Staking

Most cultivated plants require staking. This applies more particularly to hydroponic gravel culture, where the looseness of the gravel particles affords less anchorage for root systems.

Ordinary 3 ft bamboo stakes may be directly forced into the gravel, but in view of the fact that there will only be about an 8 in depth of gravel, the larger stakes, such as the 6 ft size, require tying to overhead wires.

Old boiler tubes make very useful supports for a staking system (see plate 19). These are cheap, easily obtainable from scrap dealers, and may be attractively painted.

Two sizes of tube are required. The smaller diameter tube (upright) should be able to slide into the larger one (sleeve): 1 in external diameter is suitable for the upright and $1\frac{1}{4}$ in internal diameter for the sleeves. Sleeve lengths of about 24 in are sunk into concrete at suitably spaced intervals around the tank. (See plates 16 and 19.) The 1 in pieces are fitted into these so as to stand 5 ft higher than the top of the tank wall.

The steel pieces are first wire-brushed to remove rust and scale, then painted, once with aluminium, and finished off with two coats of a glossy exterior enamel.

A system of overhead wires is slung between the steel tubes. Rust-proof hose clips are useful for securing these wires to the upright tubes. This method has the advantage of allowing the position of the wires to be adjusted at will. Plastic-coated wire is the best to use. Galvanised wire should be avoided. The bamboo stakes are tied to the wire with raffia. The plants in their turn are then tied to the stakes.

There are other ways of arranging staking systems. At the CDM installation at Oranjemund, SWA, header posts of wood are placed at intervals along the tank. Wires are strung, parallel with side and end walls, at different heights. To these the tomato plants are secured.

(2) *Rain*

Heavy rain has a twofold effect on plants in gravel. The rain beating on the gravel particles can injure lettuce seedlings and other low-lying plants. Also, excessive rainfall will flush the nutrients from the bed. If prolonged, mineral deficiencies may appear.

A light overhead screen will help to reduce the first-mentioned trouble.

The second factor is more difficult to deal with. Apart from causing a softer growth and eventually chlorotic plants, excessive rainfall dilutes the nutrient in the reservoir.

The procedure to follow during a prolonged rainy spell is to irrigate at least every second day in spite of the rain. Exceptionally long periods of rainy weather may be compensated for either by dry feeding the tank when opportunity permits or by adding a pound of extra nutrient to the reservoir. Experience in these matters is again the only guide.

The waste pipe shown in Fig 16 can also be used, during heavy rainfall, to run the drainage to waste when the reservoir is full.

(3) *Sunlight*

All plants require adequate light for satisfactory growth. Sometimes when the intensity is too great, shade has to be provided.

Plants do, however, vary in their demands. Certain crops, such as lettuce, usually require less light than the tomato, for example. Most floral crops require a reasonable amount of light.

Normal photosynthesis takes place in the presence of two different wavelength regions of radiant energy, the red and blue bands. A proper balance is provided by natural sunlight.

Light intensities are measured by the number of microwatts per sq cm of area.

The duration of light or *photoperiod* is also important. There are the short-day plants, requiring 10–13 hr of light a day, and the long-day plants, needing 14–18 hr a day.

Too high a light intensity can adversely affect the growth of some plants. For this reason outdoor plants are often shaded by palm fronds or wire gauze. Too much shade will produce a softer growth, while insufficient shade can definitely retard the growth rate and quality of the produce.

Since conditions vary from area to area, it is not possible to lay down a set of rules. Experience will dictate the proper degree of shade to use. A reduction of 25–50 per cent of sunlight will be sufficient for salad crops. With crops such as the tomato little shading is necessary.

The hot sun beating down on a dark gravel surface can produce at times alarmingly high temperatures. This is a distinct disadvantage with shallow-rooted surface crops such as radish. As plants develop, their leaves serve to shade the gravel from the hot sun. The advantages of placing down a layer of light-coloured stone over the gravel surface have already been mentioned.

One final word about sunlight. The choice of a site for the hydroponic installation is most important. The tanks must have direct sunlight. Avoid building the tanks in areas likely to be in shadow, particularly for the all-important morning light from 10 o'clock onwards. Remember that sunlight intensity can always be reduced, but it is not so easy to produce it when it is not there. Watch out for shadows likely to be cast by trees, walls or other buildings.

CHAPTER NINE

Chemical arithmetic and formulae

CHEMICAL ARITHMETIC

All material things on earth are made up of combinations of different substances known as chemical *elements*. There are over 100 of these, but in hydroponics we are only directly concerned with some fifteen. The elements themselves are composed of *atoms*, the ultimate discrete particles of matter. Each element is characterised by the weight of its atom or *atomic weight*. This is merely an arbitrary weight given to each element relative to the weight of a particular isotope of carbon which has an atomic weight of 12.

Besides its atomic weight, each element is denoted by a *chemical symbol* which is usually the first letter or first two-letter abbreviation of the name of the element. Sometimes these names are of English derivation, sometimes Latin. Potassium for example is known by its Latin name—Kalium—hence its symbol 'K'. Nitrogen has the symbol 'N' and phosphorus 'P'. Magnesium which is both Latin and English has the symbol 'Mg'—and so on.

Table 4 lists the elements commonly used in hydroponic calculations, together with their symbols, exact atomic weights and, for calculation purposes, the 'rounded-off' atomic weights.

Remember that the atomic weight is a *relative* number which could be called grammes or pounds depending on whether the metric or British system is being used.

All chemical salts are composed of *molecules,* themselves built up from units of atoms. Take potassium sulphate for example. This is one of the chemical salts used to supply the potassium in the nutrient solution. This salt is composed of two atoms of potassium, one of sulphur and four of oxygen. The molecular formula is written thus: K_2SO_4.

TABLE 4

Element	Symbol	Atomic weight	'Rounded-off' atomic weight
Boron	B	10·82	11
Calcium	Ca	40·08	40
Carbon	C	12·01	12
Chlorine	Cl	35·46	35
Copper	Cu	63·57	64
Hydrogen	H	1·008	1
Iron	Fe	55·84	56
Magnesium	Mg	24·32	24
Manganese	Mn	54·93	55
Molybdenum	Mo	95·95	96
Nitrogen	N	14·00	14
Oxygen	O	16·00	16
Phosphorus	P	30·98	31
Potassium	K	39·09	39
Sodium	Na	22·99	23
Sulphur	S	32·06	32
Zinc	Zn	65·38	65

The *molecular weight* is obtained by adding up the individual atomic weights listed in Table 4.

$$K_2 \quad S \quad O_4$$
$(2 \times 39) + 32 + (4 \times 16)$ which totals 174.

All salts, therefore, have molecular formulae and molecular weights with which the necessary amounts for the nutrient solution can be calculated.

In order to avoid confusion of thought on different systems it might be as well to discuss the point now.

The most universal of all systems of weights and measures is the metric system based on the concept of the metre, which scientists in Napoleon's day intended to be one ten-millionth part of the earth's quadrant measured from the Equator to the North Pole. Nowadays, it is the length of a bar of certain metal kept in the Archives at Paris. All measurements and capacities in the metric system are based on this.

The only facts to remember are:

1/100 of a metre = 1 centimetre (1 cm)
1 cm × 1 cm × 1 cm = 1 cubic centimetre (1 cc)
1 cubic centimetre of pure water weighs 1 gramme (1 gm)

The British system is somewhat less logical than the international metric system, which will come into force in the UK eventually, but the following facts must be known:

1 British pound = 16 ounces avoirdupois
1 British gallon of pure water weighs 10 British pounds
1 British pound = 454 grammes
1 British ounce = 28·34 grammes.

The term 'British' (or 'Imperial') is used since there are also American gallons. This unit is 0·83 of an Imperial gallon. The reader should be aware of this when making up formulae taken from American textbooks.

Parts per million concept

The concentration of salts in water can be expressed in many ways. There are ounces per gallon, milliequivalents per litre, millimoles, grammes per litre and parts per million.

This last expression, commonly abbreviated to ppm, is basically metric and capable of easy conversion to the British system. Consequently it will be adopted as the method of expression in this book.

Parts per million is the same as grammes of salt per million grammes of water or, since 1 cc of water weighs 1 gm, per million cubic centimetres of water.

It is common practice to write down nutrient formulae thus: Nitrogen 180, phosphorus 60, potassium 300 ppm.

From the foregoing it will readily be seen that nitrogen 180 ppm means that 1 million cubic centimetres of water has 180 grammes of nitrogen (in the form of a salt) dissolved in it.

The next step is to calculate how much of the salt itself is necessary to provide 180 gm of nitrogen. When it has been decided what salt is to provide the nitrogen, and take ammonium sulphate as an example, use the following procedure:

(1) Write down the molecular formula: $(NH_4)_2SO_4$
(2) Work out its molecular weight:
$$(2 \times 14) + (2 \times 4) + 32 + (4 \times 16) = 132.$$
(3) Work out the percentage nitrogen of the molecular weight:
$$\frac{(2 \times 14)}{132} \times 100 = 21 \cdot 3 \text{ per cent}$$
(4) From this percentage work out the concentration of *salt* required to give 180 ppm of nitrogen:
$$\frac{180}{21 \cdot 3} \times 100 = 845 \text{ ppm.}$$

This, then, is the amount of ammonium sulphate in grammes that must be dissolved in 1 million cc of water to produce 180 gm of nitrogen (180 ppm).

These four steps are fundamental and may be applied to calculate the amount of *any* salt required for *any* element.

Sometimes, one salt will provide more than one element. For example, ammonium dihydrogen phosphate $(NH_4H_2PO_4)$ provides both nitrogen and phosphorus for the nutrient solution. The calculation follows the same steps just given.

Once the number of gms per million cc (ppm) of salt that are required have been calculated, the next step is simple conversion of the metric to the British system. For this purpose just remember that:

1 part per million = 1 lb per 100,000 Imp gallons.

Taking the ammonium sulphate example above, 180 ppm of nitrogen is provided by 845 ppm of ammonium sulphate or 845 lb per 100,000 gallons water, ie 0·845 lb (13½ oz) per 100 gallons. This conversion brings the calculation down to terms probably more familiar to the man in the street.

The converse of the above is dealt with just as easily. Suppose a formula calls for 8½ oz of magnesium sulphate (Epsom salt) per 100 gallons of water.

The problem is to calculate the ppm of magnesium in the formulation.

First bring the concentration to lb per 100,000 gallons, ie ppm, thus:

$$\frac{8½ \times 1,000}{16} = 532 \text{ lb per } 100,000 \text{ gallons (ppm)}$$

Next, work the four fundamental steps given above, thus:

(1) Molecular formula $MgSO_4.7H_2O$
(2) Molecular weight   246
(3) Percentage magnesium $\dfrac{24 \times 100}{246} = 9·8$ per cent

(4) $\dfrac{9·8 \times 532}{100} = 52$ ppm

This, then, is the ppm of magnesium calculated from the weight of salt in ounces per 100 gallons.

Please note that some salts exist in different forms. Magnesium sulphate, for example, is found more usually as the familiar (Epsom salt) heptahydrate $MgSO_4.7H_2O$, but it is also available as the anhydrous salt, $MgSO_4$. Before calculating the ppm of an element, the exact molecular formula of the salt intended to be used must be ascertained. Another noteworthy point in this connexion is that many fertiliser grade chemicals are not 100 per cent pure, hence do not conform exactly with their theoretical molecular weights. An example of this is potassium sulphate, K_2SO_4, which theoretically has $\dfrac{78 \times 100}{174} = 44·8$ per cent K.

The commercial salt, however, is only guaranteed to contain

40 per cent K. Therefore an allowance for this lower potassium content, by using proportionately more of the salt in the mixture, has to be made.

The reader who wishes to make up his own nutrient formula might very well come across something like this (molecular weights in brackets): ·

	lb	oz
Monopotassium phosphate (136)	1	4
Potassium nitrate (101)	5	–
Calcium nitrate (236)	7	8
Magnesium sulphate (246)	3	12
Water to	1,000 gallons	

This is a formula put out by the University of California Agricultural Experimental Station. Remember here that the gallons are United States gallons and are only equal to 833 Imperial gallons.

The first step is to find suppliers of the chemicals. Then, depending on the amount required, each chemical is weighed out and dissolved in the given amount of water. It is best to add the calcium salts last of all. Also make sure that at least 75 per cent of the total amount of water is present, otherwise a local concentraion of certain combinations of elements is likely to throw down calcium precipitates. For example, if 100 gallons of solution are to be prepared, at least 75 gallons of water should be present in the reservoir before adding any salts. Never attempt to make a solution more concentrated than the formula calls for.

When single or treble superphosphate is used, there will always be more or less sediment, consisting of insoluble impurities and calcium sulphate, which takes a little time to dissolve. Simply ignore this sediment.

Should you wish to work out the theoretical ppm of the elements given in the above formula, you would arrive at the following:

N 190, P 34, K 275, Ca 152, and Mg 45.

THE IDEAL FORMULA

There is no such thing as an ideal formula. There are literally hundreds of different published formulae. From this rather staggering mass one might write out an optimum range for each of the nutrient elements.

Such a scheme might read thus:

	Minimum ppm	Maximum ppm	Optimum ppm
Nitrogen	90	200	140
Phosphorus	30	90	60
Potassium	200	400	300
Calcium	120	240	150
Magnesium	40	60	50

Two other factors play an important part in deciding what formula to use. First there are the climatic conditions. For reasons beyond the scope of this book, the potassium/nitrogen ratio is most important and should be varied with the climate. During the longer sunny summer days the plant needs more nitrogen and less potassium than during the shorter darker winter days. It is common practice therefore to double the ratio K/N during winter. This will make for harder growth in winter than would take place on a summer diet.

Second, the type of plant being grown, leafy or otherwise, has an influence on the formulation. Lettuce and cabbage would benefit from a formula with a higher nitrogen content than would be given to tomato plants, for example.

By and large, however, in the authors' experience *plants are extremely tolerant*. Nearly all plants will do well on one general nutrient mixture, with the reservations that:

(a) the pH value must be adjusted, and

(b) that winter and summer mixtures are used in the corresponding seasons, that is roughly from May to September and October to April respectively in the southern hemisphere.

130

Before leaving the major elements, it should be explained that they exist in solutions as ions, not as molecules of the salts. For example, nitrogen occurs in hydroponic solutions as either the nitrate ion (NO_3^-) or the ammonium ion (NH_4^+). It is as the ion that the element is assimilated, and while the plant absorbs either of the above nitrogen-containing ions, the NO_3^- is the one more readily absorbed. For a number of reasons which need not concern us here hydroponic solutions should not have more than 20 per cent of their nitrogen as ammonium nitrogen.

Ammonium nitrogen in the form of ammonium sulphate helps to maintain the solution pH on the acid side owing to the fact that the ammonium radical is very easily assimilated, leaving a sulphate residue which is acidic. This tends to counteract the normal alkaline drift through assimilation of nitrates and phosphates.

Phosphate is present in solution mainly as $H_2PO_4^-$ ion with some HPO_4^{--} ion. Since these ions can react with the ions of many of the metal ions, including those of the trace elements, to form insoluble salts, there can be precipitation of these to the detriment of the plant. For this reason the concentration of phosphate is purposely kept as low as possible consistent with the maintenance of an adequate supply.

Although stated to be one of the major elements, no remarks have yet been made about sulphur. This element commonly occurs in its salts as the sulphate (SO_4) radical. Many of the commercial salts used for making up the nutrient formula consist of sulphates. Fortunately, the plant is tolerant of very high sulphate concentrations. This is the reason why the sulphur concentration is not usually stated in a nutrient formula.

TRACE ELEMENTS

So far discussion has been confined to the macro elements only. It was mentioned in Chapter One that six other elements are necessary in minute amounts. These were stated to be iron, manganese, copper, boron, zinc and molybdenum, although many other elements such as aluminium, chlorine, silicon, sodium, have also been found in traces in plants.

There is more general agreement over what levels of trace elements should be supplied. Above certain concentrations, the trace elements are very definitely toxic to plants. For this reason their concentrations in the nutrient solution must be rather carefully controlled. The following list gives the minimum, maximum and optimum suggested levels of trace elements in the final nutrient solution:

	Minimum ppm	Maximum ppm	Optimum ppm
Iron (Fe)	2·0	5·0	4·0
Manganese (Mn)	0·1	1·0	0·5
Copper (Cu)	0·01	0·1	0·05
Boron (B)	0·1	1·0	0·5
Zinc (Zn)	0·02	0·2	0·1
Molybdenum (Mo)	0·01	0·1	0·02

MIXING TRACE ELEMENTS

Since the trace elements are required in such small concentrations, their compounding and mixing with the nutrient solution presents a bit of a problem, if one is not a chemist.

Many authorities advocate the use of two stock solutions of trace elements—one for iron and another for the rest of the elements.

The most practical scheme is to weigh out *ten times* the amount of each salt required to provide the recommended amount of trace element, and to dissolve this in the same 1 gallon of water. Then it is an easy matter to add 16 fluid ounces ($\frac{1}{16}$ gallon) of the single stock solution to each batch of nutrient solution.

An example will make this quite clear. Imagine working with batches of 100 gallons of nutrient solution. Step one is to calculate the amount of the particular salt required to produce the recommended amount of trace element. Suppose the iron salt is weighed out first. Ferrous sulphate ($FeSO_4.7H_2O$) is one of the salts which can be used. The recommended level is 4·0 ppm Fe. Now apply the four steps given on p 127.

(1) Molecular formula $FeSO_4.7H_2O$

(2) Molecular weight   278

(3) Percentage Fe of molecular weight $= \dfrac{56 \times 100}{278} = 20\cdot1$ per cent.

(4) Concentration of salt required to give 4·0 ppm Fe
$= \dfrac{4\cdot0 \times 100}{20\cdot1} = 20$ ppm.

But a weight which will give *ten times* this concentration, or 200 ppm $FeSO_4.7H_2O$, is required.

On the British system this would be:
200 lb per 100,000 gallons, or
0·2 lb (3·2 oz) per 100 gallons.

This is *ten times* the concentration required. On dissolving the 3·2 oz of $FeSO_4.7H_2O$ in 1 gallon water and adding $\frac{1}{10}$ or 16 fluid oz to each of ten batches of 100 gallons of nutrient solution, a final concentration of 4 ppm Fe will be provided.

Calculate the other salts of the trace elements in a similar manner.

In order to prevent precipitation of the iron in particular, during storage, add 10 cc concentrated sulphuric acid to the gallon of stock solution.

CAUTION: Always add sulphuric acid slowly to water, not the other way around.

Table 5 gives the amounts of various trace element salts to weigh out and dissolve in 1 gallon of water to provide ten additions at the recommended concentrations.

Many authorities consider the addition of molybdenum unnecessary, arguing that a sufficient amount of this trace element will be found in the nutrient solution from impurities in the chemicals used to make it up. In fact some growers go further and omit addition of all trace elements except iron. The authors recommend that at least the first five should be added. Providing

133

TABLE 5

Element	Salt	Molecular formula	Molecular weight	Per cent of Element	Amount to use per gal of water for 10 additions of 16 fl oz per ea 100 gal nutrient solution	
					oz	gm
Iron (Fe)	Ferrous sulphate	$FeSO_4.7H_2O$	278	20·1	3·2	91
Manganese (Mn)	Manganese sulphate	$MnSO_4.4H_2O$	223	24·6	0·326	9·2
Copper (Cu)	Copper sulphate	$CuSO_4.5H_2O$	249	25·6	0·032	0·91
Zinc (Zn)	Zinc sulphate	$ZnSO_4.7H_2O$	287	22·8	0·070	2·0
Boron (B)	Boric acid	H_3BO_3	61·8	17·5	0·46	13
Molybdenum (Mo)	Sodium molybdate	$Na_4MoO_4.2H_2O$	242	39·6	0·008	0·23

the pH of the nutrient solution is kept slightly on the acid side of 7·0 then all the heavy metals and iron will be found to last for that period between changes of nutrient solution.

When a dry-feed powder is being prepared, make the trace-element mixture detailed in Table 5, mixing each salt in its dry form in the proportions given (Trace-Element Dry-mix).

For every 100 parts by weight of dry macro-chemicals use 1 part by weight of Trace-Element Dry-mix, making sure that the final powder has been thoroughly mixed.

MACRO ELEMENT CHEMICALS

Before presenting actual formulae to the reader it would be useful to consider the commercial chemicals available for the various mixtures. Table 6 lists these.

TABLE 6

Element	Salt	Molecular formula
Nitrogen (Nitrate)	1. Potassium nitrate	KNO_3
	2. Calcium nitrate	$Ca(NO_3)_2.4H_2O$
	3. Sodium nitrate	$NaNO_3$
Nitrogen (Ammonium)	4. Ammonium sulphate	$(NH_4)_2SO_4$
	5. Ammonium nitrate	NH_4NO_3
	6. Ammonium dihydrogen phosphate (mono ammonium phosphate)	$NH_4H_2PO_4$
Nitrogen (Ammonium)	7. Di-ammonium hydrogen phosphate (Di-ammonium phosphate)	$(NH_4)_2HPO_4$
	8. Urea	$CO(NH_2)_2$
Phosphorus	9. Potassium dihydrogen phosphate (monobasic potassium phosphate)	KH_2PO_4
	10. Mono calcium phosphate	$CaH_4(PO_4)_2.H_2O$
	Plus 6 and 7	
Potassium	11. Potassium sulphate	K_2SO_4
	12. Potassium chloride	KCl
	Plus 1 and 9	
Calcium	13. Calcium sulphate (native gypsum)	
	Plus 2 and 10	$CaSO_4.2H_2O$
Magnesium	14. Magnesium sulphate (Epsom salt)	$MgSO_4.7H_2O$
	15. Anhydrous magnesium sulphate	$MgSO_4$

FORMULAE

Since there are hundreds of combinations of salts which could be used for hydroponic growth, only a few typical formulae taken from England, the United States and the Continent are presented for the reader's benefit.

United States of America
No 1. Summer Formula

	Gm per 100 litres	*Oz* per 100 *Imp gals*
Potassium nitrate	110	$17\frac{3}{4}$
Calcium sulphate (Gypsum)	76	$12\frac{1}{4}$
Magnesium sulphate	52	$8\frac{1}{2}$
Monocalcium phosphate (Treble supers)	31	5
Ammonium sulphate	14	$2\frac{1}{4}$
Total	283	$45\frac{3}{4}$

Provides	*ppm*
N	180
P	63
·K	410
Ca	220
Mg	50

No 2. Winter Formula

	Gm per 100 litres	*Oz* per 100 *Imp gals*
Potassium nitrate	55	9
Potassium sulphate	50	8
Calcium sulphate (Gypsum)	76	$12\frac{1}{4}$
Magnesium sulphate (Epsom salt)	52	$8\frac{1}{2}$
Monocalcium phosphate	31	5

(Treble supers)

Ammonium sulphate	14	$2\frac{1}{4}$
Total	278	45

Provides	ppm
N	104
P	63
K	410
Ca	220
Mg	50

England
No 3

	Gm per 100 litres	Oz per 100 Imp gals
Potassium nitrate	55	$8\frac{3}{4}$
Sodium nitrate	64	$10\frac{1}{4}$
Ammonium sulphate	12	2
Monocalcium phosphate (Treble supers)	44	7
Magnesium sulphate (Epsom salt)	52	$8\frac{1}{2}$
Calcium sulphate (Gypsum)	86	$13\frac{3}{4}$
Total	313	$50\frac{1}{4}$

Provides	ppm
N	200
P	88
K	200
Ca	270
Mg	50

No 4

	Gm per 100 litres	Oz per 100 Imp gals
Monopotassium phosphate	31	5
Calcium nitrate	107	17
Magnesium sulphate (Epsom salt)	58	$9\frac{1}{4}$
Ammonium sulphate	9	$1\frac{1}{2}$
Total	205	$32\frac{3}{4}$

Provides	ppm
N	145
P	70
K	90
Ca	180
Mg	58

Germany
No 5. Knop's Formula (1865)

	Gm per 100 litres	Oz per 100 Imp gals
Potassium nitrate	20	$3\frac{1}{4}$
Calcium nitrate	80	13
Monopotassium phosphate	20	$3\frac{1}{4}$
Magnesium sulphate (Epsom salt)	20	$3\frac{1}{4}$
Total	140	$22\frac{3}{4}$

Provides	ppm
N	125
P	45
K	136
Ca	136
Mg	20

South Africa
No 6. Summer

	Gm per 100 litres	Oz per 100 Imp gals
Calcium nitrate	135	$21\frac{1}{2}$
Magnesium sulphate	55	$8\frac{3}{4}$
Monocalcium phosphate (Treble supers)	47	$7\frac{1}{2}$
Ammonium sulphate	19	3
Potassium sulphate	75	12
Total	331	$52\frac{3}{4}$

Provides	ppm
N	200
P	94
K	330
Ca	305
Mg	50

No 7. Winter

	Gm per 100 litres	Oz per 100 Imp gals
Potassium sulphate	88	14
Magnesium sulphate	55	$8\frac{3}{4}$
Monocalcium phosphate (Treble supers)	47	$7\frac{1}{2}$
Calcium nitrate	85	$13\frac{1}{2}$
Total	275	$43\frac{3}{4}$

Provides	ppm
N	100
P	95

Provides	ppm
K	380
Ca	220
Mg	50

These are seven of many types of formulae available. Some will be found more suitable, under a given set of conditions, than others.

Formulae 3 to 7 cannot be stored in the dry form owing to the hygroscopic (moisture-absorbing) properties of calcium and sodium nitrate.

Certain difficulties will be encountered by the grower wishing to make up his own mixture. Firstly, not all of these salts are readily available, which is most discouraging, especially if only one salt out of the whole formula is missing. The usual sources of supply are the industrial chemical supply houses and the fertiliser firms. On a smaller scale the pharmacist might be able to help out.

Secondly, one has to have a scale to weigh out the chemicals.

Lastly, the cost of making one's own mixture, on a small scale at any rate, would be higher than that of a commercial powder.

For the beginner, and even for the larger grower, the commercial powder has much to commend it. The formula is a proven one under a variety of conditions. Since these commercial powders are made complete with trace elements, the grower avoids the bother of mixing at least ten chemicals (often a disheartening prospect).

These commercial powders store practically indefinitely provided they are kept away from moisture.

Liquid forms of nutrients are also widely used—although they tend to be much more expensive.

PART THREE

CHAPTER TEN

The cultivation of specific crops

So far this book has given details of the technique and apparatus, as it were, for practising this specialised form of horticulture. However, very little mention has been made of specific plants. After all, the ultimate aim of horticulture is the successful propagation and production of flowers and vegetables. Most gardeners, hydroponic or otherwise, are fairly familiar with normal gardening practice. Popular articles on this subject appear in the newspapers, in magazines, and on the radio.

All gardeners will recognise the familiar injunction to 'plant in a light, well-drained soil, etc.' Although in hydroponics instructions of this nature may be neglected or rather replaced with such words as 'plant in $\frac{1}{8}$ in gravel in a properly designed tank', the general gardening techniques such as disbudding, stopping, spraying, remain essentially similar. It has been mentioned before, and it is worth repeating, that hydroponics does not conflict with any natural laws—on the contrary, the science of hydroponics assists or works in with them.

For this reason, therefore, it is not the object in this chapter to offer exhaustive advice to gardeners about the cultivation of specific plants. This knowledge can be obtained from one or more of the excellent books on gardening subjects. The aim is rather to provide the hydroponic grower with gardening information on a few flower and vegetable types which can be grown well in hydroponic tanks.

Since there is virtually no competition between plants for food, it is possible to place the plants closer together within and

20 *Rooted carnations in gravel*

between rows, consistent with adequate light requirements. This factor does introduce a new aspect into crop production and is *one* of the big justifications for this method of floriculture.

It is a simple matter for anyone to plant seeds or cuttings in soil or gravel and *watch* them grow. But to produce first-class flowers or vegetables requires care, attention and a certain amount of what has been termed 'know-how'.

An attempt will be made to present this 'know-how' as it relates to the following:

FLOWERS: Carnation, gladiolus, chrysanthemum, antirrhinum and rose.

VEGETABLES: Tomato, lettuce, cucumber, pea and strawberry (fruit).

IMPORTANT NOTE

It cannot be emphasised too strongly that the following cultural notes apply to countries in the southern hemisphere, but the main difference between north and south is not in cultural detail but in seasonality. In temperate zones in the northern hemisphere summer is considered to run from May to September and winter from October to April.

142

A. FLOWERS
Carnation

Of all floral crops produced by the hydroponic method, the carnation is surely the undisputed leader. Many large installations all over the world, both under glass and in the open, are devoted to carnation cultivation.

The most popular type cultivated commercially is the American Tree, also known as the Perpetual Flowering Carnation, so-called because of its almost continuous production of blooms. The Sim variety is a very popular strain of this flower, highly cultivated by discerning growers throughout the world.

Propagation. Carnations may be produced from seeds or cuttings taken from other plants. Propagation by seed in general has already been dealt with in Chapter Six. There is little to add to this, except to mention that there is a certain amount of interesting speculation attached to growing by seed.

The one disadvantage of seed is that true-to-type varieties cannot be guaranteed nor can first-class blooms be expected, though a certain proportion might result.

Cuttings. These should be taken from healthy, carefully selected stock plants. Vigorous true-to-type parent plants only should be chosen. These are available from specialist owners.

Good cuttings are usually about 3 in long with a least four developed pairs of leaves. These should be removed from a little above the base of the plant, not from near the top. Generally, the early autumn and spring months are the best for cuttings.

A vigorous parent plant should yield eight to twelve cuttings, but no more than three should be taken at any one time. Make sure that these are neither too sappy nor too hard. Remember to remove the leaves around the node before placing in clean, medium-size, sharp quartz sand.

Although not essential, it will help to dip the prepared cuttings into a hormone preparation. After placing in sand, feed the new cuttings with a half-strength nutrient. Within 3 weeks the rooted cuttings will be ready for planting-out into their final positions in the hydroponic tank.

143

21 *Carnation 'Wm Sim' 4 weeks after planting*

Planting-out. Plant the cuttings in rows 10 in apart with a plant-to-plant spacing within a row of 8 in. Do not place the stem more than $\frac{1}{2}$ in in the gravel or sand.

Stopping. When the plant has grown to a straight stem, consisting of about ten pairs of leaves, 'stop' it by nipping the stem with a sideways pull of the fingers so that a strong stem of five or six pairs of leaves remains. This operation induces 'breaking' which is a branching out from the basal buds. Stopping is best practised during the early morning when the plants are likely to be turgid.

Five or six branches should result from the first stopping. When each of these has itself grown to about ten leaf pairs, a second stopping may take place. It is important to deal with each branch as it develops and not all at the same time. Remove the ends of the shoots in the same manner as the first stopping. This staggered method will guard against shock and promote continuity of flower production.

Staking. This is of utmost importance if plants of top quality are being grown. The carnation plant is prized for the shape and beauty of the bloom set at the end of a long sturdy stem. At all times, therefore, it is essential to give adequate support to these plants. Different growers have different ideas on how this should be

144

carried out. Some subscribe to the idea of a wire spiral of increasing radius, the spirals being themselves fixed to bamboo stakes. Note that if galvanised wires are used they must first be painted with bitumen.

Other growers use a series of bamboo stakes to which each 'break' is tied with raffia. As the plants develop, a series of wire and string at definite levels, coinciding with the ranks and files of the plants, is rigged up. This wire-string system of squares starts about 7 in above the bed and further courses are added as the plants grow, each course being about 6 in above the other.

Disbudding. For the finest blooms the carnation grower must practise 'disbudding'. This is simply the removal of buds which develop in the axils of the leaves and round the terminal bud. The object is to limit each stem to one flower only. Do not attempt to disbud until the buds are large anough to be easily handled; on the other hand, do not delay unduly, otherwise the flower will be small.

Feeding (South Africa). During the months October to February use a general summer mixture of hydroponic nutrient at full strength. The optimum pH range is 6·0–6·5. Gradually increase the potassium content from February onwards by giving mixtures of summer and winter formulations until April, when only winter mixture should be fed to the plants. As these plants are very susceptible to root rot, aim to keep the sand or gravel nicely moist and no more. During the hot summer days a light spraying of water over the foliage should prove beneficial. At all times there should be free air circulation. This is no problem in beds outdoors, but poor circulation is detrimental to plants growing under glass.

Pests and Diseases. Though not exactly a pest, mention must be made of the carnation grower's problem of the *split calyx*. The calyx of the carnation, that green portion capped around the petals, has a great predisposition to splitting, which is manifested by an unsightly bulge and untidy flowers. This nuisance can mean the difference between profit and loss to the commercial carnation grower and must be prevented before it starts. Some growers prefer rubber bands placed firmly around the developed bud, others use plastic ties. It is essential, however, to be aware of this factor and to guard against its occurrence.

The carnation is susceptible to a great variety of pests and diseases. Table 7 lists them, with appropriate counter measures.

TABLE 7

Aphids	BHC, demeton-S-methyl, derris, diazinon, dichlorvos, dimethoate, formothion, malathion, nicotine, oxydemeton-methyl, parathion, propoxur, schradan
Earwigs	BHC, DDT, DDT/BHC
Red spider mite	azobenzene, demeton-S-methyl, derris, diazinon, dichlorvos, dicofol, dimethoate, oxydemeton-methyl, parathion, quinomethionate, schradan, tetradifon, tetradifon/malathion
Rust	mancozeb/zineb, thiram, zineb
Thrips	BHC, DDT, DDT/BHC, derris, diazinon, dichlorvos, malathion, nicotine
Tortrix	DDT, DDT/BHC, dichlorvos
Wilts	benomyl
Woodlice	BHC, DDT, DDT/BHC, parathion

See note, p182.

The important thing is constant vigilance and a regular prophylactic spraying programme. Remember always to make sure that the *underside* of the leaves are sprayed, especially for red spider. Carnation growers vary their spraying cycle to 7, 10 or 14 days. It is beyond the scope of this discussion to go into detail on pests and diseases. The inexperienced carnation grower will have to learn from his own experience, together with information derived from books dealing specifically with this subject.

Carnations lend themselves particularly well to hydroponic culture. The dry-feed system in sand is to be recommended. Much care and attention, however, is necessary for success.

146

22 *Close planting of gladioli bulbs* 23 *Exquisite blooms of gladioli*

24 *Gladioli 'Allard Pierson' 6 weeks after planting*

Choose an open position with plenty of sunshine and shelter from wind. Do not over-water, and above all, be on the look-out for pests and diseases.

For culture under glass in temperate zones, select a modern light-admitting structure (see p 187) with a heating system capable of maintaining at least 50°F (10°C). Fan ventilation systems are much recommended for carnation culture in temperate zones. Note also of course the difference in seasonality in the northern hemisphere.

Gladiolus

Unlike the carnation, this charming flower requires the minimum of attention. It is most popular with hydroponic growers, but unless assured markets at steady prices can be obtained, the profit margin at certain times of the year can be very low or even non-existent. However, for the amateur hydroponic grower, the gladiolus is always a popular floral crop. Many commercial growers are more concerned with producing corms for resale than cut flowers.

Gladioli corms are available in varying sizes. The extra large corms are generally cultivated by the exhibition growers, for whom the size and beauty of the individual spike are of prime importance. Medium size corms are suitable for most purposes.

Planting in the Tank. First dig a shallow trench about 4 in deep into the growing medium. Place the corms in a straight line with about $\frac{1}{2}$ in between each. Leave about 6 in between rows. Replace the medium over the corms and smooth over with the hand, but do not compact. At this spacing 3,500 corms of medium size can be planted in a tank 4 ft × 50 ft. With smaller corms the total would be nearer 5,000.

In favourable weather mature corms will show above the surface of the gravel within 10 days to 2 weeks; some will be quicker, others slower. After their first appearance the plants grow at a tremendous rate. Dudley Harris has recorded growth rates of at least 1 in a day in $\frac{1}{8}$ in gravel.

It is not necessary to feed the young plants with full-strength nutrient solution immediately, but there is no harm in so doing. Gladioli will do well on a general mixture at pH 6·0.

Since the corms are rather susceptible to fungal rot, particularly in fine or poorly drained media, they should never be over-watered.

With gladioli as the sole crop it is a comparatively easy matter to arrange a 'drier' irrigation schedule. Mixed crops growing in a tank present more of a problem. Here a compromise is the only solution.

The gladiolus likes warmth and should be planted from August to December (February to May in northern temperate latitudes). The flowering period varies from 80 to 90 days after planting. By stagger-planting every 2 weeks, it is possible to obtain flowers for almost 6 months of the year.

The spacing mentioned above is subject to a certain amount of controversy, but when one bears in mind the facts that (*a*) in hydroponic cultivation there is virtually no competition for available nutrient, and (*b*) the gladiolus is a tall flower with a leaf system more or less confined to one plane, the wisdom (?) of close planting becomes more apparent. Add to this the fact that plants will tend to mechanically support each other.

The one disadvantage is that it is more difficult to spray closely spaced plants, but this can be overcome with a little care.

The three main pests/diseases attacking the gladiolus are gladiolus fly, thrips and rust. The first two may be controlled with 'Malathion' 50% Emulsifiable Liquid and the last one with various fungicides.

The lofty spikes of the gladiolus tend to make the plant top-heavy and easily blown about by the wind. It is therefore imperative to rig up some sort of support for these plants, particularly in windy areas. One method is to arrange stakes on either side of the terminal plants in each row. Cord is tied to each stake, thereby providing a two-cord support for every plant in the row. Sets of cords can be arranged at 9 in heights.

Flower spikes should be picked in the late afternoon and at a stage when the bottom flower of each spike is just fully open.

After all the spikes have been cut, allow at least 4 weeks to elapse before lifting the corms. It is not necessary for the leaves to die back completely. Observe whether the roots have shrunk or not. If so, then cut the stems off about 1 in above the corms; remove the old corms, dust with 5 per cent BHC powder and store in a cool place with free air circulation. The original corms are grown primarily for their quality blooms, which one can expect the first season. The next season they should be grown for the production of corms rather than flowers.

Chrysanthemum

The chrysanthemum is a genus of the great family of daisies, known as the Composites. There is a great variety, from the enormous giants usually grown for their exhibition qualities, down to the singles and pompons which are smaller in size and produce many more flowers.

Broadly speaking the following methods of culture are involved:

(1) *Earlies* – which are rooted from cuttings under glass, transferred to frames, for planting out in late spring, September or April/May for southern and northern hemispheres respectively, to flower out of doors without protection. A modification of this is to provide temporary protection in the autumn in temperate zones, which usually means from September onwards in the UK.

(2) *Lifters* – in temperate zones the plants are removed as before, grown out of doors for the summer and then 'lifted' into a heated greenhouse to flower.

(3) *Direct Planted* – under glass – when the plants are grown entirely with the protection of a greenhouse.

(4) *Spot and Year Round Cropping* – when the photoperiod of the chrysanthemum plant is exploited by a system of lighting and shading to lengthen or shorten the days accordingly.

(5) *Semi-Direct* – a variation of the above, when the plants are grown for a time outdoors before being planted under glass.

150

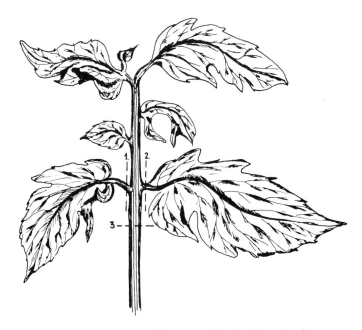

Fig 24 *Original chrysanthemum cutting showing trimmings*

(6) Pot growing of spray varieties can also be carried out on a
spot or year round basis, using soil-less media.

In all cases involving direct, semi-direct, spot and year
round, single and double and treble stem growing can be involved,
although in modern terms most commercial growers now
concentrate on single stem cropping. Either standards (large
bloom) or sprays (called American Sprays) are involved in all
cases.

Cuttings. Although chrysanthemums may be grown from seed,
most growers, especially the exhibition aspirants, are interested in
propagating true-to-type. For this purpose the cutting, similar
in many respects to the carnation cutting, is the best method of
plant production.

Cuttings strike easily in coarse sand fed with nutrient and

25 *Golden 'Princess Anne' chrysanthemums 4 weeks after planting*

grow into sturdy plants.

Cuttings are best made in early spring from the sucker growths—those growths with small roots on old crowns. When the sucker growth has reached about 5 in in height, cut the stem with a sharp knife just below a node. (See Fig 24.)

Trim the cutting by removing the two side leaves and squaring off just below the joint.

The cutting is then firmly placed in sand after dipping in a plant growth hormone powder and watered with half-strength nutrient solution until rooting has taken place. This should occur within a month, so that by the end of September, the plants should be ready to set out in the gravel tanks, where they should be spaced 6–12 in apart.

Owing to the highly specialised nature of chrysanthemum culture in modern cropping techniques, readers are strongly advised to seek detailed advice from a specialist work on the subject (eg *Chrysanthemums – The Year Round,* by Searle & Machin, or *Complete Book of the Greenhouse,* by Ian G. Walls).

TABLE 8

Aphids	BHC, demeton-S-methyl, derris, malathion, oxydemeton-methyl, schradan
Caterpillars	DDT, derris, TDE
Earwigs	BHC, DDT, TDE
Leafminer	BHC, diazinon, parathion
Powdery mildew	copper, dinocap, quinomethionate, sulphur
Red spider mite	demeton-S-methyl, derris, diazinon, oxydemeton-methyl, schradan, tetradifon

See note, p182.

Pests and Diseases. Chrysanthemums are susceptible to a variety of diseases and Table 8 above lists methods of control.

Antirrhinum

The antirrhinum or, to give it its more popular name, the snapdragon, is a prolific flowering annual which does wonderfully well in gravel beds. It yields its delightful flower spikes for many months.

The easiest method of propagation is by seed. Plant in vermiculite seed-trays as instructed in Chapter Six. When the seedlings have grown to two leaf pairs and are about $2\frac{1}{2}$ in high, they may be transplanted directly into the gravel beds.

Seeds may be germinated all the year round, though February/March for winter flowering and September/October for summer flowering are the best times to sow. These recommendations apply to South African culture. In temperate zones sow in January/February for planting under glass in March/April or out of doors in May.

Some varieties grow rather tall, so that proper staking is essential.

This plant is rather susceptible to rust so that regular spraying with anti-fungal spray is recommended.

Irrigate with the general mixture at pH 6·0.

Rose

Pride of place among all the flower kingdom may be said to go to the rose. Although as old as history itself, the modern rose is a blend of European and Eastern varieties—of which China provided the greater part.

The preparation of soil and the planting of the roses therein is a veritable ritual occupying quite a few pages of any book dealing with this subject. In the hydroponic method, planting is as simple for roses as it is for tomatoes.

There are many types and varieties of roses, but for convenience these may be divided into three broad classes, namely:

(1) the Hybrid Teas;
(2) the Polyanthas; and
(3) the Floribundas

We shall deal exclusively with the Hybrid Teas, the familiar rose bush, grown for pleasure and exhibition, by the majority of gardeners.

Planting. When received from a nursery, the young rose bush will consist of *stock,* which are the roots and stem, to which the *scion* has been grafted. The stem extends up to 2 in above the roots where the scion or potential bud stock commences.

Planting may take place in the southern hemisphere between the beginning of August and end of September. A short dormant period occurs in January when roses may also be planted. In temperate northern zones plant out of doors October/April or under glass in January.

Dig a hole in the gravel about 18 in in diameter and 6 in deep. (In soil one has to dig the hole at least 18 in deep.) Place the plant into the hole so that the root system is completely covered. Spread the roots by hand so that they comfortably fill the available space. Irrigate with the general summer mixture at pH 6·0 as soon as possible.

Space the plants at least 2 ft from plant to plant and 1 ft from the sides of the tank. A 4 ft × 50 ft tank at this spacing would accept 48 plants.

As soon as the bush has established itself, the shoots will grow very strongly and within a short space of time the original bare bush will be a mass of green leaves and developing buds.

Pruning. Outdoor pruning should be done when the plant is dormant—July in South Africa, March in temperate northern zones. Plants under glass in the UK should be cut back after planting.

Always cut at a 45-degree angle parallel with and about $\frac{1}{4}$ in above an *outward* facing bud. Use a sharp pair of secateurs and make a clean cut. The idea of choosing an outward-facing bud is to encourage the new shoot to grow outwards. Very soon after pruning, paint the newly exposed surface with aluminium paint. This is to seal the wound and discourage fungal die-back.

After pruning, the bush should consist of a neat, roughly circular spread of bare branches, each with its buds awaiting to shoot when spring arrives.

Disbudding. The same principle applies to roses as to standard chrysanthemums or carnations. The elimination of all but one bud, where more than one is competing for the available sap, encourages a more vigorous flower. Exhibition growers have to pay particular attention to disbudding if they wish to obtain the desired results.

In short, roses grow extremely well in gravel using the sub-irrigation method. Growth is more vigorous than usual, necessitating a bold pruning programme.

Owing to the relatively shallow depth of the hydroponic tank, staking is essential.

Since the plants are perennials it will not be possible to sterilise the gravel during the time it is occupied by the roses.

Pests and Diseases. Table 9 shows these and methods of control.

TABLE 9

Aphids	BHC, demeton-S-methyl, derris, dimethoate, formothion, malathion, nicotine, oxydemeton-methyl, schradan
Black spot	captan, dodine, mancozeb/zineb, maneb
Caterpillars	DDT, derris, trichlorphon
Leafhoppers	DDT, malathion
Powdery mildew	dinocap, dodemorph
Red spider mite	demeton-S-methyl, derris, dimethoate formothion, oxydemeton-methyl, schradan, tetradifon
Rust	mancozeb/zineb, maneb
Scale insects	malathion, petroleum oil
Slug sawfly	BHC, derris, lead arsenate
Thrips	BHC, DDT, derris, malathion

Other flower crops

There is almost no limit to the variety of flowers which can be grown in gravel. For commercial purposes, however, one is limited to flowers fetching a reasonable price on the available markets. Purely for the joy of growing, however, the reader may sow seeds of any flower he may fancy. Those already grown by Dudley Harris have been mentioned in Chapter Seven. Sow, for example, the seeds of the dahlia, cactus and other varieties. You will be overjoyed at the results. The second year, if you so wish, you can plant the tubers which have formed from your original dahlia seedlings.

Grow some sweet peas, stocks, marigolds, delphiniums, zinnias—they will all provide you with colour and variety.

Do not be afraid to experiment. Remember that the hydroponic method allows much scope. Begin by growing at controlled pH values. Try different media. Vary the irrigation schedules etc.

Pot plants

Before leaving the subject of flowers, a brief mention of the

26 *Hydroponic troughs of Gerbera, gladioli, chrysanthemum and carnations*

hydroponic method with pot plants should be made.

All over the world, the number of flats has multiplied tremendously to keep pace with the ever-growing population. Where before stood spacious homes with gardens are now vast concrete complexes—familiar flats or apartments.

The urge to grow plants is inherent in all, though perhaps less opportunity exists for the flat-dweller. But pot-plant cultivation seems to be the perfect answer.

With the hydroponic method, using vermiculite, lignite or peat, the bother of preparing special potting soils is eliminated.

Pot plants such as the African violet, begonia, cyclamen, coleus, dieffenbachia, caladium, primula, peperomia, sanseviera, to name but a few, may be cultivated with little trouble.

Window-boxes, arranged on decorative stands, or pots may be used as containers. Prepare them for holding vermiculite exactly as described in Chapter Four. If plastic containers are used, painting is unnecessary.

Feeding may be carried out either by the dry-feed or the solution method. The latter requires storage facilities but is preferable.

Imagine the pleasure to be derived from the yellow and gold foliage of the lofty dieffenbachia; the proud blossom of the

157

27 *Tulips 'Golden Trophy', and 'Orange Sun' in hydroponic bed*

amaryllis; the quaintness of the peperomia; the homeliness of the neglected coleus.

For convenience a list of the more popular. pot plants is appended in Table 10.

TABLE 10

Name	Description of foliage or flower
Aphelandra	Handsome variegated foliage, red or yellow flowers.
Coleus	Very popular, multicoloured foliage.
African violet (St Paulia)	Noted for their attractively coloured flowers in hues of violet and white.
Begonia (Rex)	A most handsome foliage in several varieties.
Cyclamen	Noted for their delightful blooms.
Caladium	Fancy leaves in greens and pinks.
Dieffenbachia	Yellow and gold foliage.
Gloxinia	Gorgeous blooms in red/white and purple/white.
Philodendron	The 'Delicious Monster', very decorative foliage.
Peperomia	Beautifully patterned leaves.
Sanseviera	Mother-in-law's Tongue, decorative spiky foliage.

158

The more familiar bulbous plants, such as amaryllis, hyacinth, tulip, daffodil, gladioli and crocus may all be cultivated hydroponically indoors in vermiculite and lignite.

Do not overwater bulbous plants. Remember that the bulbs themselves have quite a reserve of food, so that overfeeding should also be avoided.

Each of the plants listed in Table 10 has its own preference for more or less humidity, light, water and so forth. Some plants, such as cyclamen, may be started from seed; others, such as the African violet, are very easily propagated from the leaf.

Experience in the UK and America has shown that an almost endless range of pot plants can be grown successfully in materials of high capillarity, such as vermiculite, lignite, and of course soilless media. Once again readers are referred to any one of the many excellent books on pot-plant culture, and provided one feeds regularly, cultural methods of growing in soil or aggregates are in many ways largely similar.

Pests and Diseases. These, and their cures, are listed in Table 11.

TABLE 11

Aphids	BHC, BHC/tecnazene, demeton-S-methyl, derris, diazinon, dimethoate, formothion, malathion, nicotine, oxydemeton-methyl, parathion, schradan
Botrytis	benomyl
Powdery mildew	benomyl
Red spider mite	demeton-S-methyl, derris, diazinon, dimethoate, oxydemeton-methyl, parathion, schradan, tetradifon, tetradifon/malathion.
Scale insects	diazinon, malathion, parathion, petroleum oil.
Vine weevils	BHC, DDT.

See note, p182.

B. VEGETABLES

Under the average conditions of supply and demand it is not a commercial proposition to raise the ordinary vegetable crops by hydroponic methods, especially under glass. Where extraordinary conditions prevail, however, such as in isolated desert or inland areas where transport is poor or lines of communication long, hydroponically grown vegetables are a commercial possibility.

It is the authors' opinion that hydroponically grown vegetables, apart from tomatoes and cucumbers, under *ordinary conditions of marketing*, cannot compete with normal methods of vegetable crop production. So often, however, do extraordinary conditions (eg scarcities through drought or pests) prevail, that there are times when this generalisation is not valid.

Tomato

Tomato growing is a specialised subject. Suitable reading is *Tomato Growing Today* by Ian G. Walls.

The tomato is a vegetable that lends itself admirably to hydroponic culture, especially when one considers the problems of 'soil sickness' which arise in conventional soil culture, and when one realises that it is necessary to maximise output almost on a 'production line' basis to survive in the European Economic Community, especially in the UK.

The tomato is a native of a coastal plain in South America where temperatures are generally around 59° F (14·0° C) at night and 66° F (18·9°C) by day, and the light intensity, although high, takes the form of diffused rather than direct sunlight. While the tomato can be grown outside in temperate zones, it is much more suited to greenhouse conditions, and in Europe it is invariably grown as a warm glasshouse crop.

Seed Sowing. Tomatoes are raised almost exclusively from seed, which is sown in vermiculite, perlite, lignite or peat at 65° F (18·3° C) day and night temperatures. After a few days in darkness, germination takes place, and the little seedlings are ready for 'pricking off' in 10–14 days in good light conditions.

While in South Africa tomatoes can be grown more or less

160

on a year round basis, with more emphasis on the summer season (October–April), in temperate northern hemisphere zones it is usual to sow seed for the early crop in November or December for planting in February, and at intervals for successively later crops, until March or early May for the late crop. Considerable savings in time can be achieved by the use of either 'growing rooms', where all light is supplied artificially, or 'supplementary light', where natural light is added to by either mercury vapour, fluorescent or sodium lamps on a double batch basis. Full details of these techniques are readily available in the UK from Electricity Boards or specialist books on the subject.

Potting or Planting. In temperate northern latitude zones it is usual to pot up the seedlings into pots of varying sizes from $3\frac{1}{2}$ to $4\frac{1}{4}$ in and many varying composts. For those anxious to adhere to hydroponics right through the whole cultural process, vermiculite, lignite or even sand can be used, although peat or peat/sand media are highly successful (see p 40). It is important to feed constantly with nutrients, using complete spectrum types or, alternatively, if *base feeding has been used in the media* (with the trace elements), the following mixture used both at the potting and the cultural stage.

TABLE 12

	Composition of feeds (oz/gal)		Nutrient (per cent weight/vol) (approx)	
K_2O to N ratio	Potassium nitrate	Urea or Ammonium nitrate	K_2O	N
3:1 (High Potash)	24	–	–	6	2·0
2:1 (Standard)	24	5	6	6	3·0
1:1 (High Nitrogen)	24	16	20	6	6·0

Note: this stock solution is prepared by careful mixing in warm water. It is diluted to 1 in 200, usually with a calibrated dilutor. If using a watering can, the dilution is 1 fl oz of stock solution in $1\frac{1}{4}$ gallons of water. *Note that this is used where complete base feeds containing trace elements are supplied.*

Under warm conditions where the cost of heating is not a critical factor there is certainly virtue in planting seedlings direct into hydroponic beds, but in temperate zones it is not considered to be economic, certainly not for the early crop, the situation being entirely different in May or June under glass.

Growing Procedures. The basic make-up for hydroponics culture can take several forms, either going completely over to tanks or, in recent years in temperate zones under glass, into troughs constructed of polythene. Trenches set in the ground can also be used, provided drainage is not restricted. The selected aggregate is put in the trough or trench, and while one can include peat culture, the base exchange capacity of peat and to a lesser extent perhaps lignite can work for or against the gardener. Shortages of vital elements can occur through 'lock-up' where base exchange mechanism operates, but conversely the effect of excess nutrients is nullified.

In Britain Mr Walls has very successfully grown tomatoes in simple polythene-lined trenches with coarse lignite 8 in deep and 8 in wide, with side drainage holes 2–3 in from the base. A base dressing of Vitax Q4 was applied at the rate of 8 oz per sq yd and N, P, K enriched Maxicrop used from the outset. The first trial of this system at a nursery at Timperley in Cheshire involved a batch of tomato plants and gave results commensurate with tomatoes grown alongside in steam-sterilised soil.

Such simple systems involving materials of high capillarity such as lignite and vermiculite would seem to offer excellent scope for the gardener or grower unwilling to become too deeply involved in complicated and expensive types of hydroponic systems. The same system has been applied in other experimental work using 4 ft wide beds, 8 in deep, again with drainage facilities in the side of the trench to work this sub-irrigation system.

Mr Harris has described dry feed systems basically similar to the above which have proved highly successful with sand. At the Agricultural Development and Advisory Service at Bognor Regis in Sussex and at the Glasshouse Crops Research Institute constant flow systems of tomato culture, where nutrients are circulated through small polythene troughs (see plate 29), have given excellent results, but it must be pointed out that nutrient

162

adjustment and replacement as described earlier (see p 92) still apply. The reader will appreciate, therefore, that within the broad hydroponics context several different systems of culture can be indulged in, and the system must obviously be decided upon before the plants are either set out as minute seedlings in limited quantity or left in propagating cases for planting out in their growing quarters.

Planting Distances. In general, planting distances allow for a plant density of 12,000–16,000 per acre, which in round figures means an allowance of 2·8–3·6 sq ft per plant. In very approximate practical terms this means plant spacing of 14 × 22 in or thereabouts according to circumstances. In 4 ft troughs with 2–3 ft between them the plant will obviously require 14 × 14 in in double rows each way to get the given density per acre. At all events planting must not take place until the temperature of the media is at least 56°F (13·3°C).

Training. Obviously the tomato plants require support from the outset; the commonest method in Europe is to tie polypropylene tissue around the neck of the plant and secure it to wires running across the greenhouse structure. The plants are either trained vertically or obliquely, or vertical growing early in the season is combined with dropping or layering the plants later. Side shoots are removed to maintain a single cordon and bottom leaves removed up to the ripening trusses.

Feeding and Watering. The tomato plant has a tremendous capacity for water from as little as 2 pints per week in dull weather when young up to 3 gallons or more per week when the plants mature. Constant nutrition is also required to sustain growth on a constant supply basis, taking care to flush out salts when there is any evidence of salt damage. The nutrition of tomato plants is complex in the extreme and requires judgement to maintain a balance between potash and nitrogen, something which can be done by varying the feeds detailed earlier according to circumstances.

Tomatoes can form up to 12—24 trusses under glass with good management, with yields varying from 5–6 lb per plant to 24 lb per plant, and very high yields have been achieved in aggregate or 'semi-hydroponic' systems (in peat or peat/sand) in many countries over the last 10 years. Mr Harris has obtained 900 lb from a 4 × 50 ft trench (9 lb per plant) out of doors in South Africa.

It must be emphasised once again, however, that the economics of hydroponic culture of tomatoes, particularly under intensive glasshouse culture, revolve around a readily repeatable system and successional crops, ie early crops followed by later ones without the high cost of a trough system fitted with steam lines to sterilise the media.

There can be successive cropping in a temperate zone, the early crop planted in February being replaced by a late crop planted in July.

Varieties. Varieties are legion and vary according to requirements. Earliana, Houtbaai and other varieties not available in the UK are good for early cropping. Possibly the best known variety in Britain is Eurocross BB and one of the most recent Hollandbrid.

Pests and Diseases. The tomato is prone to a number of pests and diseases. Most serious is perhaps virus, now offset to a large extent by the virus innoculation technique to bring forward the check period. Botrytis disease is another danger, but several chemicals, of which benomyl, a systemic fungicide, has given excellent results, can counter it successfully. Table 13 lists pests, diseases and remedial measures:

TABLE 13

Aphids	BHC, demeton-S-methyl, derris, diazinon, dichlorvos, dimethoate, malathion, nicotine, oxydemeton-methyl, parathion, propoxur, tecnazene/BHC
Botrytis	benomyl, dichlofluanid, dicloran, tecnazene, tecnazene/BHC
Brown root rot ('Corky disease')	chloropicrin/dichloropropane-dichloro-propene/methyl isothiocyanate, dazomet, metham-sodium, nabam, zineb

164

Leafhoppers	DDT, DDT/BHC, malathion
Leaf miner	BHC, DDT/BHC, diazinon, nicotine, parathion, tecnazene/BHC
Leaf mould (*Cladosporium*)	benomyl, copper, maneb, nabam/zinc sulphate, zineb
Potato cyst eelworm	chloropicrin/dichloropropane-dichloro-propene/methyl isothiocyanate, dazomet, dichloropropane-dichloropropene,dichloro-propene, metham-sodium
Red spider mite	azobenzene, demeton-S-methyl, derris, diazinon, dichlorvos, dicofol, dimethoate, oxydemeton-methyl, parathion, petroleum oil, quinomethionate, tetradifon, tetradifon/malathion
Root knot eelworm	chloropicrin/dichloropropane-dichloro-propene/methyl isothiocyanate, dichloro-propane-dichloropropene, dichloropropene, parathion
Springtails	BHC, DDT/BHC, diazinon, tecnazene/BHC
Stem rot (*Didymella*)	captan
Symphylids	BHC, parathion
Thrips	BHC, BHC/tecnazene, DDT, DDT/BHC, derris, diazinon, dichlorvos, malathion, nicotine, tecnazene/BHC
Tomato moth	DDT, DDT/BHC, dichlorvos
Whiteflies	BHC, BHC/tecnazene, DDT, DDT/BHC, dichlorvos, malathion, parathion, propoxur
Woodlice	BHC, DDT, DDT/BHC, parathion, tecnazene/BHC

See note, p182.

Lettuce

Lettuce is perhaps the most important salad vegetable after the tomato. It is both nutritious and forms an attractive addition

165

28 *Young tomatoes growing in gravel*

29 *A constant-flow system of tomato culture*

THE CULTIVATION OF SPECIFIC CROPS

30 *Developing carnations in Dudley Harris's sub-irrigated tank*

to any salad dish. There is nothing to compare with the clean crisp heads of lettuce which may so easily be grown in gravel beds.

Essentially a cool-weather crop, lettuce may, however, be cultivated throughout the year, especially in temperate climates under glass, although it will be necessary to shade the plants during the hot summer months in warm climates. The optimum growing temperatures range from 55° to 75° F.

Lettuces are best started in vermiculite seed-beds. The seedling may be transplanted into gravel or sand when the second pair of leaves is about an inch in size. The best time to transplant is in cool cloudy weather or towards evening. A protective shade-cap is recommended until the transplant has become acclimatised in hot weather. The older leaves often wilt and wither somewhat after transplanting, particularly where they have been in contact with the hot gravel, but this condition does not really harm the plants. It is often possible to plant the seedlings between older tomato plants so that their foliage provides shade for the developing lettuces.

Transplant at a spacing between plants of 8–10 in. A 4 ft × 50 ft tank would hold just under 300 lettuces at this spacing. If the grower is producing for his own table, he should stagger his planting so as to ensure an almost continuous supply of fresh lettuce.

Although the optimum pH preference for the lettuce is reported as 7·0, a pH of 6·0 gives excellent results.

A general mixture, fed once daily during the summer months, will produce mature heads in 8 weeks or less after transplanting. During the cooler winter months growth is naturally slower.

The variety known as 'Great Lakes' gives excellent results in both gravel and sand.

The above notes on lettuce growing apply to culture out of doors in a warm climate, typifying growing systems which have been developed because of arid weather or poor soil conditions. Under glass in temperate zones it is doubtful whether the cost of setting up hydroponic systems would be economically justified with such a low value crop, which can, in any case, be grown well in soil. A wide range of varieties, including 'short day' types, are available in Europe. In recent years 'growing room' raising of lettuce plants in soil blocks has been much practised commercially—seedlings are given 10 days of continuous light at 500 lumens and are subsequently planted out and grown on a production line basis—and obviously there could be advantage in this successional cropping pattern on hydroponic beds, as growth can be very rapid.

Pests and Diseases. See Table 14 for these and curative measures:

TABLE 14

Aphids	BHC, demeton-S-methyl, derris, diazinon, dimethoate, formothion, malathion, nicotine, oxydemeton-methyl, tecnazene/BHC
Botrytis	benomyl, dicloran, tecnazene, tecnazene/BHC, thiram
Downy mildew	mancozeb/zineb, thiram, zineb
Rhizoctonia	quintozene
Springtails	BHC, DDT/BHC, diazinon, nicotine, tecnazene/BHC
Symphylids	BHC

See note, p182

Peas

Like the lettuce, this is a comparatively easy crop to grow in sand or gravel.

Gravel-grown peas are both deliciously sweet and tender. The reader should make a point of growing some for the table.

Place the seed directly into the gravel about 1 in deep, at a spacing of about 4 in between plants. Planting times vary in different areas of South Africa for the early crops, but seeds for the main crop should be planted in the period July–September for picking about 3 months later.

As it is rather a difficult job staking peas, it is best to allow them to grow on to a trellis or some sort of rot-proof netting, where the tendrils may entwine themselves for effective anchorage of the plant. They must be adequately supported, otherwise drooping and consequent contact of foliage with the medium will occur.

The pea is subject to fungal infections in warm, moist conditions. This can be prevented by spraying with a suitable fungicide.

Pick the pods as soon as they are fully formed. It is not good practice to leave them on the plant after their complete development.

It is doubtful in temperate zones whether one would be justified in growing garden peas under glass, apart from an early crop of a dwarf variety sown in northern temperate latitudes in January or February with a minimum temperature of 50°F (10°C).

Cucumber

Unlike the lettuce, cucumber is a warm-weather crop and grows very well in gravel, providing the plants are given a little attention. Cucumber belongs to the family of Cucurbitaceae, of which watermelon, sweet melon and pumpkin are also members.

Either plant the seeds directly in the gravel during August to January, or transplant from vermiculite seed-beds. The germination period is rapid. It is best to grow the plants near the edge of the tank at 15 in intervals and train the vines at an angle to overhang the edge. In this manner there will be plenty of space for the fruit to hang down, while at the same time it will be possible to intercrop with lettuce or some low-growing vegetable.

Within 3 months of planting, the fruit, which, like most hydroponically raised vegetables, is of first quality and full-flavoured, can be harvested.

The cucumber is rather susceptible to frost, so due precautions should be taken against this.

Another weakness is mildew infection, which is encouraged by warm, moist conditions. Avoid wetting the foliage but, at the same time, ensure that the roots are adequately watered at least once daily in the summer months.

Use a general summer nutrient at pH 6·0.

The cucumber in temperate zones is essentially a glasshouse crop for dependable results, although it can also be grown in frames or out of doors. It certainly can be grown in hydroponic beds, but preferably supported with strings on a single cordon system (like tomatoes) to make best use of space. Constant flow nutrient solutions, as practised with tomatoes, are excellent for cucumbers. Timing in temperate northern latitude zones will be sowing from December till March for planting January–April, although. later crops can be taken. Being light-demanding, production will be very difficult in the winter months in northern Europe and countries of similar latitude. Many modern varieties including 'all female' types have now been developed.

Pests and Diseases. See Table 15 for a list, plus counter measures to use:

TABLE 15

Aphids	demeton-S-methyl, derris, diazinon, dimethoate, malathion, nicotine, oxydemeton-methyl, parathion, propoxur, schradan
Botrytis	benomyl

'French fly'	parathion
Millepedes	DDT (to beds only), parathion
Powdery mildew	benomyl, copper, dinocap, quino-methionate, sulphur
Red spider mite	azobenzene, demeton-S-methyl, derris, diazinon, dicofol, dimethoate, oxy-demeton-methyl, parathion, petroleum oil, quinomethionate, schradan, tetra-difon, tetradifon/malathion
Rhizoctonia	quintozene
Root knot eelworm	dichloropropane/dichloropropene, parathion
Root maggot	parathion
Springtails	BHC (to beds only), diazinon, nicotine
Whiteflies	malathion, parathion, propoxur
Woodlice	BHC, DDT (to beds only), parathion

See note, p182.

Strawberries

Though strictly falling into the category of fruit, it will be convenient to deal with strawberry culture here.

The red succulent strawberry is a universal favourite, especially as the season is so short.

The plants may easily be cultivated in gravel or sand. One disadvantage is that, whereas it is normal to leave the plants in the soil after fruiting, it is not convenient to follow the same practice in hydroponic tanks.

Procure some stock plants. Plant into the tanks 6 in apart and 6–8 in between rows. A 4 ft × 50 ft tank will accommodate at least 500 plants. Planting time is June to August for fruiting in December to January.

In northern latitude temperate zones planting is in October-November under glass for fruiting in April-May according to the level of heat given. Best results follow from night temperatures of 55° F (12·8° C) and day temperatures of 60–65° F (15·6–18·3° C).

171

Deblossomed runners established in small pots are generally used as planting material, and are removed after fruiting to make way for other crops under glass, but can of course be left to grow on in outdoor tubs or beds. The first crop will be light, but the crop can be highly rewarding commercially due to its early arrival. If plants are left, they will fruit at a higher level the second time of fruiting, which will be in a period of 3–4 months according to weather. Two crops of certain varieties can be taken under glass in temperate zones. It is important to ensure first quality plants, free from troubles such as virus or eelworm. Varieties most favoured for early culture in Europe are Gorella and Glasa. Good control of the environment is essential under glass to avoid fruit rots caused by botrytis. Regular feeding at a fairly high level, with a pH of 6·0, is generally successful, but feeding levels must be related to growth rates.

The use of a barrel to grow strawberries is also practical. The barrel, bored with a series of 1 in holes at approximately 1 ft intervals, is filled with sand or vermiculite. The plants are placed in the holes and the contents of the barrel watered from above. Eventually, from the plants which have been planted in the holes, fruit will hang down the sides of the barrel.

Variety of Crops

The crops which have been briefly described are but a few of those which can be successfully grown under hydroponic systems. Indeed it is the joint opinion of the authors that provided there is a sensible approach to nutrition, almost any crop can be grown to perfection.

Crops in Polythene Bags

Experiments with crops using polythene bags have shown that this method of growing has some merits.

The object of growing in polythene bags is three-fold:

(a) the gravel in the tank does not become blocked with fine roots;

(b) the advantage of portability; and

172

(*c*) certain pests such as cut-worm are discouraged.

Instead of planting the seedling directly into the gravel, it is placed into a medium, which could be gravel, sand, vermiculite or perlite, within a double polythene bag. The bag will vary in capacity according to the size of the plant being grown, but a 12 in length by 6 in diameter would be suitable. Fill the double bag with the growing medium, pierce several small holes around the sides with a kitchen fork and place the filled-out bag into a hole dug in the gravel in the tank. About an inch of the top of the bag can stick out above the surface of the gravel.

After the crop has been harvested, it is a simple enough matter to screen out fine roots from the gravel and so keep the greater proportion of the gravel clean.

The technique of growing tomatoes in polythene bags filled with soil-less media, generally peat/sand, has been carried out successfully for many years in Ireland and the UK.

CHAPTER ELEVEN

How to beat pests and diseases

The gardener has indeed many hurdles to overcome before he can be said to have won the race. Probably the most troublesome are the pests and diseases which beset the plant.

At the outset please dispel any ideas that hydroponic conditions somehow endow plants with a type of immunity to pests and diseases. Many people, surprisingly, have this strange notion.

Hydroponically grown plants are unique in many respects, but this is not one of them. They are subject to the same range of pests; they fall prey to the same collection of diseases. There are, however, a few new factors which influence their incidence and prevention.

Firstly, garden soil can become contaminated with organisms that cause disease, and, once this has occurred, it is no easy matter eliminating them. In soil-less culture, by the sub-irrigation method, one starts off with freshly sterilised growing medium, pumps, pipe-lines and reservoir. (This will be explained later.) The chance of disease, corresponding to the soil-borne variety, is thus very small. On the other hand, should some alien bacteria or fungal spores find their way into the hydroponic reservoir, they are effectively spread throughout the whole tank area.

Secondly, it is a garden maxim that healthy plants are more able to withstand attacks of disease than less healthy plants. There is no doubt that, providing they are grown in the correct manner, hydroponically raised crops are healthy.

Apart from sterilisation procedure, which will be described in detail, it is intended only to discuss the broad principles of spraying, mentioning certain disease and pest types, and suggesting simple measures for their control or elimination. The finer details of this subject are dealt with in most garden manuals.

STERILISATION OF GROWING MEDIUM

After a year or two of growing crops in gravel (or sand), disease-producing micro-organisms can accumulate, thereby increasing the tendency for disease of future crops. In other cases, diseased conditions could have occurred before the end of a particular crop. In both events, chemical sterilisation will be necessary.

The technique of sterilisation by sub-irrigation is so simple, inexpensive and effective, that it might almost be recommended as a standard procedure. Chemical sterilisation will only control the common soil-borne diseases, which are introduced through the root system. By the same token, chemical sterilisation can only be practised when plants are not present, since the concentration of chemicals used would also harm them.

The best time to sterilise is between crops approximately once a year.

Chemicals Used

Although several types of chemicals are in general use, namely formaldehyde, metham sodium, cresylic acid, phenols, methyl bromide and others, the first named, owing to its availability and cheapness, is the obvious choice.

Formaldehyde is a gas which is obtainable from wholesale chemical supply companies or from pharmacies as a 40 per cent solution in water under the trade name of 'Formaline'.

The fumes of 'Formaline' are extremely pungent, so great care must be exercised when handling this material. With larger quantities it is advisable to use rubber gloves.

A 1:100 dilution of 'Formaline' in water or 4,000 ppm of active formaldehyde is the recommended working concentration.

The following is a description of sterilisation procedure for the hydroponic tank detailed in Chapter Seven for use on a large scale.

Step 1 – Fill the 300 gallon reservoir with tap water to about the 250 gallon mark.

Step 2 – While circulating the water, as described under 'Mixing the Plant Food' on p 92, slowly pour in 3 gallons of 'Formaline'.

Step 3 – With tap water, top up to working level (270 gallons) and circulate for another 10 min to ensure thorough mixing.

Step 4 – Leaving valve 1 open and valves 2 and 3 closed, operate the pump until the solution just covers the surface of the gravel.

Step 5 – Stop the pump. Close valve 1. Allow the solution to stand in the tank *overnight*. It is even more effective if the whole surface area is covered with canvas or polythene.

Step 6 – Drain the solution back into reservoir after opening valves 1 and 2.

Step 7 – Pump all the liquid in the reservoir to waste.

Step 8 – Fill the reservoir with tap water, flood and drain the tank. Pump washings to waste.

Step 9 – Repeat Step 8 twice more so that only a very faint smell of formaldehyde is left in the medium.

For small-scale sterilisation the same dilution rates apply (1 part Formaline to 100 parts water), 18 gallons of *diluted* solution being required per square yard of bed.

This procedure will sterilise not only the gravel, but also the tank surfaces, pipe-lines, valves, pump and reservoir. Large commercial installations may follow the same procedure, scaling everything up proportionately. When sterilising media in glasshouses in the presence of other plants, it is advisable to cover the tanks being sterilised with polythene or canvas.

With more porous or finer media it will probably be necessary to wash with water at least four times.

Do not sterilise old vermiculite and other porous materials such as old lignite. Firstly, being so porous, it would be an extremely tedious task washing out the last traces of formaldehyde. Secondly, old vermiculite being physically unstable (flaking of lamellae), would not be suitable to use again even if it were to be properly sterilised and washed. Lignite can, of course, be put through a riddle, using only the larger particles.

The phosphate treatment of calcareous media

Though not really connected with sanitation, it is logical to mention here the procedure to be followed for the pretreatment of calcareous gravels.

Many sands and some gravels contain shell or limestone. This consists of calcium carbonate, which if left untreated would raise the pH and cause precipitation of phosphates, iron and manganese from the nutrient solution. Any new sand or gravel must be tested for carbonates by adding dilute hydrochloric (not sulphuric) acid to a small amount in a beaker or cup. An effervescence of gas shows the presence of a carbonate. The quantity may roughly be judged by the intensity and duration of the effervescence. A gravel shown to contain more than 10 per cent carbonate, calculated as calcium carbonate, will have to be pretreated.

With a few minor differences, the procedure follows the same lines just given for formaldehyde sterilisation of gravel.

Use a strong superphosphate solution, made by adding 3 lb of superphosphate (8·3 per cent P) to every 100 gallons of water in the reservoir. Mix for $\frac{1}{2}$ hr and allow to stand overnight before use. The pH of this solution should be below 5·0 and the phosphorus content at least 250 ppm P. Pump this solution into the gravel and allow to stand overnight. Gradually the limestone and shell will be coated with insoluble phosphate and the phosphorus content of the solution will decrease.

After this soaking, drain the solution to waste. Pump the gravel with tap water, drain. Repeat the washing.

The gravel (or sand) will now be adequately treated and ready for planting.

If necessary, sand beds may be pretreated with superphosphate solution added from above.

PESTS AND DISEASES

The number of pests and diseases rivals only the number of remedies on the market for their destruction and control.

So bewildering are the numbers (of pests and diseases on the one hand, and remedies on the other) that the home gardener is justifiably driven frantic by the number of combinations and permutations in this field. An additional complication is that one particular remedy may be marketed under several trade names!

Where then does one reasonably begin and end?

The most logical approach is to decide first of all whether it is a chewing or sucking pest, and then, if possible, go further and identify the pest by consulting books, leaflets or advisory services before seeking the most suitable control measure from an authoritative source.

Technique of Spraying

Before discussing pests, diseases and their control in more detail, it is as well to have some knowledge of the technique of spraying.

Spraying does not imply simply putting a powder or liquid in the spray reservoir, adding water, and aiming it at the plants. A little knowledge about the spray materials, their compatibility, concentration, toxicity, etc, makes for more intelligent spraying with far more effective results.

Most of the spray types mentioned later are made up with water either as *emulsions* or as *wettable powders*. An emulsion is physically similar to milk—a suspension of very finely divided globules of oil in water. These sprays usually contain the active ingredient, plus an emulsifier, dissolved in an organic solvent (if liquid) or an inert carrier and wetting agent (if solid).

The object of spraying is to produce a very fine mist of spray material which will adhere to the leaves, particularly the undersides, and stem of the plant above the growing medium. The insect pests will be killed on contact or after sucking the poison. Certain modern sprays are known as *systemic*. These are absorbed

178

into the plant sap itself, thereby rendering the whole plant poisonous for 2–3 weeks. Although intended for the smaller sucking insects such as aphids, they also help to control certain virus diseases carried by these insects.

Systemic insecticides, like most other sprays, are very toxic in concentrated form to humans. Should any be spilt on the skin it must *immediately* be flushed off with water. This applies to most of the modern insecticides, which should always be stored in a safe place away from children and foodstuffs. All manufacturers are compelled by Government regulations to state the chemical composition of their product. Where necessary, handling precautions, compatibility, symptoms of poisoning and antidotes must also be mentioned. In the UK full details of all chemicals are given in the Agricultural Chemicals Approval Scheme booklet *Approved Products for Farmers and Growers*, published annually and available through officers of the Advisory Services or through HM Stationery Office.

Always adhere as closely as possible to manufacturers' instructions regarding concentration and usage. Sometimes an increased concentration of spray in water may cause permanent damage to plants.

Certain sprays are incompatible one with another. In such instances, when both have to be used, it is not always possible to mix the two different types. On the occasions when two different sprays are called for, rather spray with the one and complete the job with the other.

Avoid spraying during windy or rainy weather. The best time is on still days, preferably during early morning or late afternoon. Avoid spraying during the heat of the day.

If small hand-sprayers are used, measure the capacity of the reservoir in pints or millilitres by filling with water and pouring into a measuring device. Should the capacity be 1 pint (570 ml), for example, and diluting instructions on the label call for 2 teaspoons per gallon of water, then a $\frac{1}{4}$ teaspoon of the remedy in the 1 pint reservoir will be the correct concentration. Do not use more than instructed.

179

Types of pests

There are two main divisions of insect pests, namely the CHEWING and SUCKING insects. Table 16 lists the principal types commonly found. Some not relevant in temperate zones are marked with an asterisk.

TABLE 16

Chewing	Sucking
Beetles	Ants (indirectly)
Caterpillars	Aphids
Crickets*	Bugs
Cutworms	Fruit fly
Grasshoppers*	Red spider
Grubs	Scale insects
Locusts*	Thrips
Moths (larvae)	White fly
Slugs	

The chewing group of pests is responsible for destruction of foliage, flowers and stem, by chewing or nibbling. This is a particularly destructive group and must be ruthlessly destroyed, since it can cause rapid damage of crops.

The sucking insects are smaller in size. They pierce the plant tissue and suck the sap, thereby causing discoloration and, if left uncontrolled, eventual death.

Types of disease

When discussing the growing of specific crops in Chapter Ten, certain disease types were mentioned.

Diseases are generally more difficult to control than insect pests. In the first place they are much more difficult to diagnose, and, in the second place, once they have obtained a firm grip on the plant, they are very difficult to eliminate.

180

It is for the second reason that regular spray programmes are embarked upon for their prevention rather than for their elimination. With insect pests one can more easily see the pest and arrange for its elimination.

Plant diseases are conveniently divided into three main types, namely FUNGAL, BACTERIAL and VIRUS.

Fungi are responsible for most of the diseases of plants. These fungi are themselves plants but, unlike green plants, do not possess chlorophyll and therefore require organic nutrients. They are found in dead organic remains or on living substrates and they have a remarkable reproductive capacity by means of spores.

These fungi, which are plant parasites, establish themselves on their hosts by the spores, either air- or soil-borne, germinating and producing a germ tube which penetrates the outer cell layer of the plant and spreads germs throughout the plant body. The host plant suffers debility and may eventually die.

Bacteria are responsible for a number of plant diseases, some of which are quite devastating, but there are fewer diseases of this type than are produced by fungi.

Virus diseases are widespread in plants but seldom result in death. However, infected plants seldom grow as well as healthy plants and in some cases, eg potato viruses, the crop can be reduced by 75 per cent or even more. More and more virus diseases are found annually and their significance increases. Often virus and insects are intimately associated, the insect transmitting the virus from plant to plant. Viruses are not capable of reproducing away from their hosts, although they are often very sensitive to external agents like sunlight and other environmental factors; they are remarkably persistent.

The treatments used in the control of plant disease are basically preventive. There are two types. The most widely used are sprayed on to the leaf surface, killing germinating spores there before they plunder the plant tissue. The same type of chemical can be partly curative, arresting further development of the fungal mycelium (the absorptive organs of the fungus). In more recent years chemicals applied either to the foliage or soil (or both) are absorbed into the plant tissue and spread throughout the plant matter and act from within the plant in a similar way to the first type. The other main preventive measure is plant sanitation. All old plants, plant debris and boxes which have had plants in them should be removed, destroyed, or cleaned, and this applies also to a greenhouse structure.

Modern plant breeders have introduced resistances and tolerances to many plant pathogens and rigorous steps are taken to produce and maintain clean stocks of fruit, flowers and vegetables.

Pest and disease control

The situation regarding the use of pest- and disease-controlling chemicals has undergone considerable revision in the UK and is referred to earlier, the chemicals available being listed in *Approved Products for Farmers and Growers* (see Tables 7–14). Some confusion still exists concerning those available to professional and amateur growers, although generally speaking and in the interests of safety, only those products in small packs freely available through amateur supply sources should be used by amateur gardeners. This by no means cancels out the need for strict care with all chemicals, whether available to amateurs or professionals. Tables 7–11, and 13–15 have been used by kind permission of the Ministry of Agriculture, Fisheries and Food, and list the chemicals available in 1974.

CHAPTER TWELVE

Climatic control

The predominant theme in this book has so far been the control of growth—standard growing media, standard nutrients and, one would therefore hope, standard results. Obviously, however, one cannot even begin to approach such a 'horticultural utopia' without giving due consideration to the climatic pattern, whether one is discussing culture with or without soil. While outdoor culture in predictable low latitude climates is one thing, and the protection of a greenhouse may only be for rain or wind, a vastly different situation prevails in higher latitudes, both north and south of the Equator. In Britain and countries of similar temperature pattern it would be impossible to think of predictable results without the use of a greenhouse provided with a system of heating and ventilation to enable a temperate climate to be maintained throughout the year. It could be further said that with the high investment necessary for a fairly complicated hydroponic system, year round culture would be more or less a necessity on economic grounds. This obviously is of less importance where only hobby or amateur gardening is concerned. A greenhouse is simply a device, largely composed of glass or other material, which allows the passage of solar radiation (or heat) and light.

TYPES OF GREENHOUSE

An immense range of greenhouses is available today, compared to the more 'standard' design of 40–50 years ago, when they were either totally steel, totally wood, or a combination of these two basic materials, and glazing systems were almost entirely based on small panes of glass retained by putty. Indeed there was more concern about stability than transmission of light and heat from the sun.

Nowadays, in almost direct contrast—although with modern technology not to the extent of loss of stability—greenhouses are constructed from a wide range of materials, such as *superior wood* (Western red cedar or oak), pressure-treated soft woods, alloy, galvanised steel, and a combination of galvanised steel and alloy. Glazing systems are now, in the main, either of the 'dry' type, the glass being retained in grooves, or plastic seals with alloy clip and 'bar cap' retaining seals. A predominant theme is to maximise the glass area and minimise the opaque material.

There are two almost quite separate industries in countries such as Britain where glasshouses are widely used. The commercial glasshouse manufacturer invariably tends to concentrate on large structures for commercial growers, the emphasis being on low cost design to give maximum coverage of land at reasonable cost, combined with design factors allowing maximum transmission of light and adequate ventilation, the whole structure being readily adapted for automation.

Commercial sizes of glasshouses vary from the 10 ft 6 in width module (called the Venlo or Dutch light structure), where an internal framework of galvanised steel supports a wooden or alloy glazing system, utilising large panes of glass (5–6 ft $\times$ $2\frac{1}{2}$ ft), up to massive wide span structures with internal steelwork and alloy glazing up to 60–70 ft wide or more. In recent years the ultra wide span structure has tended to lose favour on the grounds of high initial and maintenance costs, to be replaced by blocks of Venlos or Double Venlos of 21 ft.

Within these broad design categories exist numerous variations. One should study the products of the commercial glasshouse manufacturers, ensuring in the first place that one obtains the broadest possible picture of glasshouse design and all it involves from a horticultural consultant, as costs can vary enormously. The importance of glasshouse design and the need to pay heed to such issues as roof angles and orientation (see p 186)

184

cannot be overlooked in northern latitudes, where light is at a premium during the dull winter months. This is particularly true where the British commercial glasshouse industry is in stern competition with its fellow EEC countries, some of which are much more favourably placed climatically for light reception.

The amateur glasshouse industry, while not completely separate in all cases, concentrates on the supply of structures of a size and design suitable for amateur gardening purposes, there obviously being some overlap in design or purpose with certain Dutch light structures. An excellent range of structures is available, constructed either of superior or treated timber, alloy or galvanised steel, at highly competitive prices. There are, in addition, some firms which look more to 'local authorities' for their business, and offer greenhouses of fairly sophisticated design but well overpriced for strictly commercial purposes. It cannot be emphasised too strongly, however, that glasshouses, their design, construction and adaptability for automation are beyond the scope and intention of this book.

The following are the main issues of importance.

Site Selection

In temperate climates it is highly important to select a site allowing unobstructed solar light and energy for the majority of greenhouse crops, except for some aspects or periods of propagation, and even then only for intermittent periods. Light is the life-blood of all growing plants, and while light intensity and its attendant solar radiation may well be above the necessary levels for some of the summer months, there is the whole year to consider, and one can easily provide facilities for shade during the periods when light intensity levels are too high. Trees, buildings and hedges must all be taken into consideration. Light intensities are also better in areas free from industrial pollution of the atmosphere, or where there is a large expanse of water to reflect the light.

Exposure

It is difficult sometimes to compromise between unobstructed light and exposure. A flat treeless site may be excellent for light transmission, but if it is blasted by uninterrupted wind, the glasshouse structure itself will suffer and heat loss may be more or less doubled by the passage of cold air over the glass. Nevertheless there are many excellent sites where the presence of trees or the general topography of the land renders shelter to a certain degree without excluding the vital light; and within the level of the sites available careful consideration should be given to this issue. Frequently low-lying sites tend to be frost pockets into which cold air flows, especially during radiation frost periods, and while this will involve fairly heavy temporary demands on heating systems, the advantages of the frost pocket as a shelter usually outweigh any disadvantages.

Site Levels

Whether sites are flat or not will only be of real consequence where a large glasshouse unit is concerned, and site levelling may be necessary, as flat cropping areas are much to be preferred. The main issue with hydroponic systems will be drainage and not preservation of the soil, something which would be of paramount importance with conventional cultural systems. Indeed it could be said that quality of soil is of absolutely no importance at all— a further advantage of hydroponic systems in that 'standard' conditions for culture can be reproduced irrespective of soil quality, the variations in which can be enormous. Drainage does require careful consideration, however, as does the linking on to a suitable outlet *without causing pollution problems*—less important where plant nutrition is concerned than when using chemicals for pest and disease control or soil sterilisation. Only the last named operation is likely to use chemicals in sufficient quantity to demand a drainage outlet.

Considering the Selection of Greenhouses

Orientation and Configuration. A highly important issue with

186

all greenhouses is their shape and configuration in relation to aspect. Light in the northern hemisphere is southerly, the converse being true of the southern hemisphere. Glass, apart from allowing the passage of light waves, is highly reflective and will only transmit to its maximum when the light rays strike the glass at an angle of 90°. Obviously with the rising arc of the sun from morning until night and the further differential brought about by season, it is a question of ensuring that the best possible presentation of the maximum area of glass is obtained throughout the full year.

It has been shown by trial and research over many years that east/west orientated single glasshouses (with the apex running east/west or nearly so) transmit more total light on average over the full year, simply because this orientation presents the maximum glass surface to the sun. While it was thought that for blocks of houses north/south orientation was most feasible over the full year, recent experimentation work has shown that an east/west orientation is still the best. All this is particularly true for year-round culture in low latitude areas, a situation extremely likely when hydroponic culture is concerned.

Uneven-angled greenhouses with a steeper roof should face the south, as should mansard-shaped greenhouses which have a two-slope roof or a multiplicity of slopes to give a curvilinear effect; the latter have been developed in modern structural materials in an effort to increase light transmission.

Ventilation. It has been increasingly realised over the last few years that ventilation is a critical factor to plant growth, and certainly where one is attempting to maximise growth and provide standard conditions of growing media, as in hydroponics, it would be folly to ignore the importance of good ventilation, which of course is a vital facet of temperature control. As air is warmed, it becomes less dense and will rise above cooler air, and this natural phenomenon is the reason why most conventional ventilation systems in greenhouses allow for the escape of this warm air at the highest point in the structure. Generally, therefore, ventilators are fitted on the ridge of the greenhouse, preferably continuous on both sides of the ridge with greenhouses over 12–15 ft in width. The escaping warm air must be replaced with cooler outside air, and this is done by a combination of reciprocal interchange in the roof area and the introduction of cooler air either inadvertently through leaks in the structure or preferably by lower set vents.

Not all ventilators are, however, placed at the highest point in the ridge, many in fact being what are called full valley ventilators in the case of Venlo structures (10 ft 6 in, 3m). On one type of curvilinear greenhouse the vents are placed half way up the roof, it being assumed that the force with which either the warm air is expelled or the colder outside air is forced in by the breeze is sufficient to discharge the pocket of warm air that is trapped in the highest point of the structure, although this in practice is difficult to substantiate.

Obviously the ratio of the vent area to the floor area of the greenhouse is the critical factor, and modern research suggests that a ratio of at least one-sixth of the floor area, but preferably one-fifth, will allow sufficient air changes to keep air temperature at a sufficiently low level and avoid overheating and spoilage of the growing crops.

Humidity is also controlled to a certain degree by ventilation, it being assumed that the outside air is of lower humidity than the warm air in the greenhouse, which can hold more moisture and is consequently of higher humidity. Excess humidity, which is desirable for a certain stage of propagation, tends to encourage the development of disease in crops.

Ventilation should preferably be operated by a thermostat to open and close automatically at certain temperatures. It must be appreciated, however, that achieving the requisite number of changes under conventional ventilation systems depends much on outside air movement, and there can be many 'still' periods when it can be impossible to achieve this.

As an alternative to conventional ventilation, thermostatically controlled extractor fans will achieve a set number of air changes, usually 40–50 per hr, under all conditions. Greenhouses can also be pressurised, the air being exhausted through counterbalanced louvres, although in practice this system is less efficient than extraction. Experience in recent years has shown the real value of extraction fans, especially for temperamental flower crops such as carnations, when environmental control is a critical matter.

Heating of Greenhouses

Heat is necessary in greenhouses in most temperate climates to maintain satisfactory temperatures on a year-round basis and to assist with environmental control generally by reducing humidity. The changes which have and are taking place in greenhouse heating methods over the last decade are dramatic. While the cumbersome 4 in pipe filled with water heated by a coal-fired boiler which circulated by thermo-siphon as the lighter warm water gradually rose to the highest point in the circuit and then slowly found its way back by 'gravity' to the boiler again are still in existence, they are the exception rather than the rule. Such systems, while dependable, had a slow response, as they involved large volumes of water which took a long time to heat and cool, and that gave rise to temperature control problems. In contrast, modern systems have small diameter piping ($1\frac{1}{2}$–2 in) through which the water is generally circulated by means of pumps. The small volume of water contained in such systems can be heated much more quickly than in the earlier system, and usually with more response to changing temperatures; and in consequence these systems are more efficient in maintaining an even temperature. They have a further great advantage in their ability to disperse the pipes where heat is required instead of adhering strictly to a gradual rise and fall, although pumps can of course be fitted to larger diameter systems. The water is heated in boilers, which can be solid fuel, gas or oil fired.

Warm air heaters, either ducted or free discharge, are becoming widely used in both commercial and amateur establishments, there being a very wide range of types with varying outputs. Indeed, the simplest form of warm air heater is an electric fan heater. More recently there has been considerable interest in the use of small bore plastic pipes buried in the growing media on mist or propagation benches in lieu of electric soil-warming cables.

The whole matter of greenhouse heating tends to be specialised to the extreme, demanding careful consideration of all factors and good design, certainly where a large scale installation is concerned. It is best to deal with a heating engineer or equipment supplier *fully conversant with greenhouse heating*.

Access and Working Space

One highly important feature with all greenhouses is ready access, not only for workers but for mechanical equipment. On an amateur scale this is also important, as nothing is worse than finding it impossible to gain access with a loaded barrow or trolley, a not infrequent occurrence. Sliding doors are almost universal now in modern greenhouses.

Another issue is percentage of cropping area, a figure of 80 per cent of the total floor space being common with good planning. Adoption of hydroponic systems by no means cancels out the need for good planning so that 'beds' are of maximum size yet allow adequate movement around them for crop handling. It is a frequent fallacy that the greater the number of plants packed into a greenhouse, the higher the yield, be this tomatoes, chrysanthemums or any other crop. One would suppose that plant densities had been worked out for most crops, and while to a certain extent this is true, it is a difficult matter with the broad range of conditions which exist to be too precise.

For instance, one could plant tomatoes at 8×8 in and suffer tremendous disease problems under conventional ventilation, yet find under fan ventilation that the air movement prevented disease. The same could be true of carnations and other crops, and therefore plant densities are not a cut and dried matter and must be worked out according to conditions.

Watering Systems

There has been some discussion elsewhere in this book on watering methods, yet it cannot be stressed too strongly that it is essential to find the most acceptable watering system for any crop under the system of culture practised. With the more 'simple' hydroponic systems, watering high capillarity materials, spray lines or drip systems which are widely available on both commercial and amateur scales are ideal. However, there will be many gardeners who prefer manual watering with a hosepipe or watering can.

The dilution of liquid feeds has also been referred to previously, and one must remember that water board regulations in the UK forbid the use of dilutors directly from the mains take-off, in case feedback causes contamination. This will necessitate the use of supply tanks or reservoirs on a large scale with, if need be, the use of pumps to control the outflow. In domestic circles the house supply tank will suffice.

Greenhouse Erection

Manufacturers of both commercial and amateur greenhouses provide detailed and precise plans for self-erection. Most commercial firms also offer an erection service, and while amateur-sized houses can be self-erected, arrangements can usually be made with any competent landscape firm to erect them also.

Environmental Control

Control of glasshouse environment rests with

(*a*) control of artificial heat input
(*b*) ventilation to limit temperature rise
(*c*) control of humidity by a combination of heating,
        ventilating and watering.

Good environmental control is achieved by thermostats, preferably installed in aspirated screens (insulated boxes or large diameter PVC tubing fitted with a small fan which pulls air typical of that in the greenhouse over the thermostats). The control of greenhouse environment is by no means a straightforward issue and can be summarised as follows.

Control of Heat Input. Usually a screened thermostat situated centrally within the greenhouse regulates the temperature and calls into operation the heating system, whether this be warm water, steam or warm air. It can do this on an on/off basis or in stages. A more sophisticated way of controlling heat input with warm water systems is by the use of a close circuit adjacent to the boiler and a motorised valve, so that the temperature of the water circulated to the greenhouse is related to the amount of change in temperature registered. Conversely, when the demand for heat is satisfied, input of heat ceases or is commensurately reduced.

At the upper levels of the heat input, ventilation is usually called into action on the impulse of an aspirated thermostat, preferably in stages opening or shutting the vents according to the amount of change in temperature; and in more advanced units and in the case of continuous roof vents on both sides of the ridge (at the lee side away from the wind to avoid cold draughts) by means of a wind direction indicator. Rain gauges will also shut down vents to avoid crop spoilage. Fans are also operated by thermostats and can be variable or fixed speed according to need.

Synchronisation between heating and ventilating is essential to avoid 'hunting', although some hunting is sometimes necessary to avoid high humidity.

Humidity control, while simple in theory, is difficult in practice. Warm air holds more moisture than cooler air, the moisture being shed on glass (or plastic) by cooling. It is also deposited on the plants. Humidity, while much dependent on air temperature, is not wholly so, since the amount of water transpired by the crop is also a critical factor, as also is the amount of water evaporated from the surface of the growing media.

While raising the temperature, or, conversely, allowing the entry of cooler and presumably less moist air from out of doors, might seem the simple way of achieving humidity control, a number of variables prevent this system from working.

The raising of humidity by the introduction of water into the greenhouse by mist spray lines or mist jets set in the fans of pressurised systems (where fans pull air into the greenhouse to be extracted out of louvres) has achieved a modicum of success, as have wet pads incorporated in fans in warm countries such as California. Warm air industrial fan mist units or combined warm air mist units have also been used in an effort to achieve 'constant' environmental conditions.

Perhaps the most sophisticated controls are photometers which regulate heat and ventilation and, if necessary, humidity, by monitoring the temperature in relation to light levels, and there are many models on the market which achieve this admirably. Indeed it is true to say that possibly most environmental control systems of the future will be based on such forms of control, possibly starting with the more general acceptance of precision-growing systems based on hydroponics.

Plastic Structures

Although plastic film structures of various kinds have been used for crop production for many a decade, the late 1960s and early 1970s showed a massive increase in the worldwide swing towards their use. Britain is still very much the bottom of the plastic league, for many of the European countries, especially those in the Mediterranean area, have developed a very large plastic-growing industry. In the USA also sophisticated plastic structures are in wide-scale use. The amateur gardener, too, is beginning to accept plastic structures as a practical way of growing crops.

It is ironical that plastics were once considered as cheap glass substitutes, for the more sophisticated plastic structures can be almost as expensive as a 'conventional' greenhouse glazed with glass. This is more true of modern structures utilising rigid plastics, since their sophisticated internal frameworks are the costly items.

One vital drawback with plastic film material is its fairly rapid breakdown under the ultra-violet content of sunlight, necessitating fairly frequent renewal, particularly in an area where the sun is strong. Rigid plastic materials are also vulnerable, but less so, and in recent years most plastic materials have been given a considerable degree of inbuilt resistance to ultra-violet deterioration.

Perhaps one of the most interesting features of plastics generally is that they readily lend themselves to structures of unusual configuration which have obvious advantages as far as light transmission is concerned. All the light transmitted by plastics is diffused, not direct, but this is not of great significance to the growing plant. Indeed it might be said that the diffusion of the light is a good thing, especially in summer, although in a way plastic reduces the necessary solar heat waves. It is interesting also to note that plastics in the main, unlike glass, do not trap the reflected long heat waves, which in simple terms means a more rapid loss of sun heat.

The thermal conduction of plastic materials differs from that of glass, but for all practical purposes it can be taken as being the same when calculating heat loss, since the plastic has a 'still' layer of trapped air and film of moisture. It could be said that a plastic-film greenhouse has a lot less air leaks than a conventional glass-house, further restricting any heat loss.

Design of Plastic Structures. Basically plastic film structures are of curved design with internal framework of either galvanised steel or wood. While in the UK the plastic film tends to be stretched over the framework in a continuous film, some European structures work on a different principle—small sections of plastic are retained in hollow steel sections with blocks of wood, and plastic is lapped around circular sections with small end sections of PVC piping.

Condensation. Plastic film builds up moisture in droplet form fairly rapidly, owing to the rapid heat loss and to the fact that the moisture cools in droplets instead of dispersing as it does on glass. Treated forms of plastic film are better in this respect, but the fact remains that high humidity can be a factor of some importance, to the detriment of growing plants at certain times of year but perhaps to their advantage at propagating periods.

194

METHODS OF CONTROLLING CLIMATE

The author is frequently asked:

CAN I GROW TOMATOES OUT OF SEASON USING HYDROPONIC METHODS?'
There is an implication in this question that the hydroponic
method *per se* circumvents the laws of Nature. This is of course
untrue. The answer to the above question is: 'Provided you are
able to produce the warm and sunny condition the tomato plant
requires.' In other words, if one is able to control climatic factors
one has a means of growing plants, in theory anyway, the whole
year round. A splendid example of this is the production of
chrysanthemum blooms throughout the year by providing extra
light during the winter months and shading during the lighter
summer months.

The cost of climatic control is relatively high, and this must
always be considered in relation to the crop being marketed. It
would not be justifiable, for example, to market tomatoes in the
Western Cape from August to November unless a premium price
could be obtained. As long as sufficient light and warmth are provided, it is quite possible to grow tomatoes under greenhouse
conditions during the wetter, darker winter months prevailing in
this area.

These notes on plant physiology, while basically related to
South African conditions, are highly relevant in temperate zones.
Readers are, however, reminded that they must put them in
latitudinal context before attempting to grow any crop out of
season.

In order to understand more about the greenhouse production of crops, the three main climatic factors of light, temperature
and humidity must be considered in greater detail.

A. LIGHT

All plants require more or less light for growth. Visible light
is made up of a number of different colours manifest in the rain-
bow. The different rays are measured by their wavelengths, which

195

vary from about 4,000 Angström units in the violet to just over 7,000 Angström units in the red range.

There are three properties of light which govern its effect on plants. These are *quality*, ie the blend of wavelengths available to the plant; *intensity*, measured in watts; and *duration*, also known as the photoperiod.

Most plants require at least one-tenth full sunlight to support growth. Higher levels improve growth. At full sunlight most plants will benefit by shade. Apart from high temperatures, high intensities of light will also adversely affect growth, hence the common practice of whitewashing the glass of greenhouses during the bright summer months.

The short days of winter, especially coupled with cloudy weather, cause light to become a limiting factor in the greenhouse production of crops.

Plants may be grouped into *short day, long day* and *day neutral* with respect to the effect of the length of day on flowering.

Short-day plants need 10–13 hr of light daily to flower. Examples of these are begonias, chrysanthemums, gardenias and poinsettias.

Long-day plants need 14–18 hr of light a day. Examples are asters, coreopsis, dahlias, nasturtiums and many of the annuals grown for spring flowering.

The day neutral group includes carnations, coleus, African violets and roses. These plants will blossom as well at 12 or 18 hr of light a day.

Artificial light

Artificial light may be produced by tungsten filament lamps, fluorescent lamps, quartz mercury arc lamps, and a few other types.

Lamps must be provided with reflectors and are usually controlled by a time-clock mechanism, though manual control can be arranged as well.

The particular light installation will depend on the purpose for which it is required. If it is desired to force long-day plants to bloom earlier for a high-priced market, it may be done by extending the daylight hours with artificial light. This need not necessarily be light of high intensity. Many plants respond well up to 400 watts/m² of extra artificial light.

Conversely, short-day plants, such as the chrysanthemum, may have their blooming time extended by providing additional artificial light.

It is considered to be better practice to produce a *continuous* day of natural and artificial light rather than to have intermittent periods.

Special fluorescent lamps, claimed to produce a proper balance of the red and blue light rays, are marketed by some companies. One such lamp is the 'Gro Lux' manufactured by the Sylvania Company, Salem, Massachusetts, USA, and Thorn Lighting in the UK.

Another popular type is the Mazda lamp, which is a tungsten filament lamp available in various wattages.

Generally speaking 8–10 candelas for 4–6 hr a night should be the minimum supplied to plants.

Table 17 gives some data with respect to location, lamp size and spacing of lamps to obtain 10 candelas of extra light.

TABLE 17

Bench width (ft)	Height from bottom of reflector to bench surface (ft)	Lamp size (watts)	Lamp spacing (ft)
3	2	25	3
4	$2\frac{2}{3}$	40	4
5	$3\frac{1}{3}$	50	5
6	4	75	6

The cost of installation, as well as the cost of power, should be carefully computed before artificial lighting is installed. As far as power is concerned, inquiries should be directed to one's town council or electricity authority about the unit cost of lighting power. This is usually measured in kilowatt hours, which is the amount of electricity produced by 1,000 W in 1 hr. Thus ten

197

50W lamps burning for 2 hr would use up 1 unit at the cost prevailing locally.

In recent years the use of growing rooms, where artificial light completely replaces natural light, has come into widespread use for raising bedding plants, tomatoes, lettuce, and a whole range of propagating activities. Initially growing rooms were sophisticated units of high cost, but in modern form many involve little more than batteries of lamps in simple structures. Full details of growing rooms, precise design and use, are available from the Electricity Council, Trafalgar Buildings, Charing Cross, London.

B. TEMPERATURE

Since plants grow best within certain definite temperature ranges, control of this factor in the greenhouse is most important.

It is good practice to operate a greenhouse with a differential between average night and day temperatures. This difference is normally 10° to 20° F.

There is a general division into cool- and warm-season crops. Lettuce can be classed as a 'cool' crop with a night temperature of 50° F (10° C) and a day temperature of 60° F (15·6° C), tomatoes or peppers as 'warm' with night temperatures of 60° F (15·6° C) and day temperatures of 66° to 70° F (18·9° to 21·1° C).

By the proper regulation of air temperature in a greenhouse, growth may be controlled to a certain degree. A small increase in temperature tends to cause more rapid, softer growth, whereas a lowering in temperature has the opposite effect.

During the warm summer months, particularly during the daylight period, it is desirable to be able to cool the greenhouse. Partial shading or water sprayed around the paths will help in this direction.

Each type of crop presents its own specific problem. Temperature control for the hyacinth would present quite a different problem from that for the tomato.

198

31 *Use of artificial light to force growth*

C. HUMIDITY

Atmosphere that is saturated with water vapour is said to have a 100 per cent humidity. Half saturation would be 50 per cent or, as it is said, the *relative humidity* would be 50 per cent at a given temperature.

All plants, in the act of transpiration, lose water through their leaves. Since this is directly affected by the relative humidity of the atmosphere, its control in the greenhouse is important.

The production of an adequate humidity plays a key role in the successful rooting of cuttings.

One of the best ways of increasing humidity is to install special nozzles which inject a fine mist into the greenhouse. This system can be automatically controlled by a device known as a *humidistat*, the analogue of the thermostat.

Humidistats work on the principle of a moisture-sensitive substance which, below a given humidity setting, breaks a current and operates a relay, which activates a solenoid valve connected to the nozzles. Mist propagation is a most useful device, especially in the summer months when low humidity conditions prevail.

Since temperature and humidity are interdependent, light shade in a greenhouse will also act in raising the humidity by lowering the temperature.

32 *Thermostat ensuring a constant temperature*

33 *Extraction fan, artificial light and shading cloth in
chrysanthemum production*

In this respect it is interesting to note that a relative humidity of 80 per cent at 68° F (20° C) would only be 44·5 per cent at 77° F (25° C).

Relative humidity is easily determined by noting the difference between the dry-bulb and the wet-bulb thermometer readings. The latter is wetted by a wick dipping into water. The degree of evaporation, hence the cooling effect on the wetted bulb, depends on the relative humidity. The lower the humidity the

34 *Internal view of greenhouse. Note*
staggered vertical supports for
longitudinal tubes

greater the cooling effect. A table provided with the wet-and-dry bulb thermometer enables the gardener to read off, at a glance, the relative humidity.

The disease factor is often a greater hazard under greenhouse conditions. The reason for this is that warm, moist conditions are optimum for many, particularly fungal, disease organisms. Carnations, for example, are far more susceptible to rust, tomatoes to leaf mould, and so on. Insect pests, too, tend to multiply more rapidly. For instance, an outbreak of red spider on carnations can spread within 24 hours throughout the greenhouse. Sanitation is therefore of utmost importance.

A recent piece of modern equipment is the electric vaporiser, which effectively delivers an insecticidal aerosol, as well as fungicides, into the greenhouse atmosphere.

AUTOMATION

Greenhouse automation has now been brought to a fine art. Several American firms manufacture equipment to control mechanically just about every controllable factor in the greenhouse.

201

35 *'Maximum–minimum' (left) and 'wet-and-dry bulb' thermometers*

Such a system is the 'Ventender' Greenhouse Automation System manufactured by the Integrated Development and Manufacturing Company, Chagrin Falls, Ohio, USA.

This system provides 'Week-end Weather Protection' for the unattended greenhouses, with an Automatic Ventilator control. Beside this there are wind and rain controls, which in the event of high wind or rain automatically close the vents to a preselected position. When the adverse conditions abate, the vents return to the previously set thermostat. In the event of return to automatic control being made only by manual resetting, a limit control action is also provided.

Anemometer and rain signals are fed into the electronic control unit containing a contact meter relay which indicates rain velocity. When wind velocity reaches the limit selected, the relay causes the power unit to close the vents to a preset position. A timer inspects the conditions once a minute. When wind speed drops below the limit, the relay returns to normal and the elec-

202

tronic control unit returns to temperature control. The rain grid, when short-circuited by the rain, operates in a similar manner.

There is really no limit to the number and ingenuity of control systems which might be installed in a greenhouse. This same company also manufactures controls for light intensity, light accumulation, and carbon dioxide supplementation.

Such terms as aspirated sensing element mount, single automatic controller, circulating pump assembly, compartment junction box, automatic ventilator control, remote temperature indicator control panel, will become household words to the gardener of the future.

Another concept in automation is the Plant Growth Chamber or Environmental Laboratory.

These are cabinets of varying sizes, roughly the shape of a large refrigerator, which contain fluorescent or incandescent lamps as the source of light, fans for air circulation, as well as cooling and heating devices. These chambers allow for wide limits of light, temperature and humidity control. Built-in alarms with some models provide visible and audible notice of any control point departure.

The Environmental Laboratory is used mainly by horticultural research and plant pathology workers. They are in use in their hundreds in the United States, mainly at the universities, but also at the numerous agricultural experimental stations with which that country abounds.

GLOSSARY

Aerobic: living and functioning on air

Algae: lower form of plant life

Angström unit: a very small unit of measurement equal to 10^{-10} of a metre

Anhydrous: without water

Asexual: reproduction not involving fertilisation

Axillary bud: side shoot growing out between leaf stem and main stem (axis)

Bed: popularly used synonomously with 'tank' in which plants grow

Bituminised: painted with bitumen

Break: a side shoot

Calcareous: containing lime

Chlorophyll: green colouring matter in plants

Chlorosis: showing signs of yellowing

Conductivity: a measure of the electrical conducting capacity of water due to dissolved salts

Cutting: a side shoot from a plant for propagation purposes

Dry-feed: the application of nutrients in dry, powder form

Emulsion: an intimate mixture of water and oil of milky appearance

Flume: a narrow open channel for conducting liquid

Galvanised: coated with zinc

Gravel: material larger than 2 mm in size, up to $\frac{3}{8}$ in

Hydroponics: word coined to denote growing plants in liquid, popularly used to describe all forms of growing without soil

Humidistat: a device for controlling humidity

Humus: the broken-down remains of plants and animals forming the familiar blackness of soils

Hygroscopic: absorbs moisture

Ions: charged atoms of which salts are composed which separate when dissolved in water

Major elements: the six main plant nutrient elements; nitrogen, phosphorus, potassium, calcium, magnesium and sulphur

Medium: the material in which the plant grows, eg gravel, sand, vermiculite

Metabolism: process whereby the plant builds up nutritive material into living matter or breaks down complex into simpler substances

Minor elements: the nutrient elements required by the plant in traces only. (Not a desirable term)

204

Nutrient: mixture of major and minor elements vital to plant's growth and development

Osmosis: the passage of water through a semi-permeable membrane, eg through root hairs into the plant because of differing concentrations

Petiole: leaf stalk

pH value: a measure of acidity or alkalinity of a solution

Photosynthesis: production of sugars by plant's chlorophyll through action of sunlight

Protoplasm: life-giving fluid filling plant cells

Relative humidity: the percentage of moisture vapour in atmosphere compared with a saturated atmosphere

Reservoir: container for nutrient solution

Respiration: the breaking down of sugar by oxidation and the uptake of oxygen and release of carbon dioxide

Sand: material between 0·1 to 2 mm in size

Silt: material between 0·002 to 0·05 mm in size

Soil-less culture: popularly used synonymously with hydroponics

Stomata: tiny apertures mainly on underside of leaf allowing movement of gases into and out of leaf

Stopping: the removal of a growing point

Sub-irrigation: irrigation from underneath, usually through a channel

Sump: a small temporary reservoir

Systemic: entering plant's system or cell sap

Tank: structure, usually concrete, holding growing medium

Thermostat: a device for controlling temperature

Toxic: poisonous

Transpiration: evaporation of water through stomata; cf perspiration in humans

Vermiculite: a mined micaceous material heated in a furnace and screened to size, used as a growing medium

APPENDIX I
CONVERSION TABLES

1. LINEAR MEASURE

Metric

10Å	=	1 μm
1,000 mμ	=	1 μm
1,000 μ	=	1 mm
10 mm	=	1 cm
100 cm	=	1 m
1,000 m	=	1 km

British

12 in	=	1 ft
3 ft	=	1 yd
1,760 yd	=	1 mile

Metric to British

1 mm	=	0·03937 in
1 cm	=	0·3937 in
1 m	=	$\begin{cases} 39\cdot37 \text{ in} \\ 3\cdot281 \text{ ft} \\ 1\cdot094 \text{ yd} \end{cases}$

British to Metric

1 in	=	$\begin{cases} 25\cdot4 \text{ mm} \\ 2\cdot54 \text{ cm} \end{cases}$
1 ft	=	0·3048 m
1 yd	=	0·9144 m
1 mile	=	1·6093 km

2. SQUARE MEASURE

Metric to British

1 sq cm	=	0·1550 sq in
1 sq m	=	$\begin{cases} 10\cdot764 \text{ sq ft} \\ 1\cdot196 \text{ sq yd} \end{cases}$
1 ha	=	2·4711 acres

British to Metric

1 sq in	=	6·4516 sq cm
1 sq ft	=	0·0929 sq m
1 sq yd	=	0·8361 sq m
1 acre	=	0·40468 ha
1 sq ml	=	259 ha

3. CUBIC MEASURE

Metric to British

1 cc	=	0·061 cu in
1 cu m	=	$\begin{cases} 35\cdot135 \text{ cu ft} \\ 1\cdot308 \text{ cu yd} \end{cases}$

British to Metric

1 cu in	=	16·387 cc
1 cu ft	=	0·02832 cu m

4. CAPACITY

Metric

1,000 ml	=	1 litre

British

20 fl oz	=	1 pt
8 pts	=	1 gal

APPENDIX I: CONVERSION TABLES

Metric to British

1 litre = {
35·2 fl oz
1·759 pts
0·22 gal
}

British to Metric

1 fl oz	= 0·02835 l
1 pt	= 0·568 l
1 qt	= 1·136 l
1 gal	= 4·546 l

5. WEIGHT

Metric

1,000 g = 1 kg
1,000 kg = 1 tonne

British

437·5 gr = 1 oz
16 oz = 1 lb (avoir)
112 lb = 1 cwt
2,240 lb = 1 ton (long)
2,000 lb = 1 ton (short)

Metric to British

1 kg = {
2·204 lb
35·27 oz
}

British to Metric

1 oz = 28·35 g
1 lb = 453·6 g
1 ton (short) = 0·90718 tonnes (metric)
1 ton (long) = 1·01605 tonnes (metric)

OTHER USEFUL CONVERSIONS

1 tonne (metric) = 2204·62 lb
1 long ton of water = 35·8 cu ft
1 gal of water = 10·0 lb
1 British gal = 1·20094 US gals
1 US gal = 0·83268 British gals
1 cu ft = 6·25 gal

Oz per gal x 6·25 = gms per litre
ppm = lb per 100,000 gals or mgms per kg
1 acre = 4,840 sq yds or 43,500 sq ft
1 grain per gallon = 14·3 ppm

ABBREVIATIONS USED IN ABOVE

Å	= Angstrom unit	lb	= pound
cc	= cubic centimetre	m	= metre
cm	= centimetre	mg	= milligram
cwt	= hundredweight	ml	= millilitre
fl	= fluid	mm	= millimetre
ft	= foot	mμ	= millimicron
gal	= gallon	oz	= ounce
g	= gramme	pt	= pint
gr	= grain	ppm	= part per million
ha	= hectare	qt	= quart
in	= inch	sq	= square
kg	= kilogram	yd	= yard
km	= kilometre	μ	= micron
l	= litre	μm	= micrometre

APPENDIX II
THEORETICAL PERCENTAGES
OF SOME WATER-SOLUBLE SALTS
USED IN HYDROPONICS

	N	P	K	Ca	Mg
Ammonium phosphate, di-H	12·1	27·0			
Ammonium phosphate, mono-H	21·2	23·4			
Ammonium nitrate	35·0				
Ammonium sulphate	21·2				
Calcium nitrate	11·8			17·0	
Calcium sulphate (Gypsum)				23·2	
Magnesium sulphate (Epsom salts)					9·9
Potassium dihydrogen phosphate		22·8	28·7		
Potassium nitrate	13·8		38·6		
Potassium sulphate			44·8		
Sodium nitrate	16·4				
Superphosphate (single)		8·3		18·0	
Superphosphate (treble)		21·0		14·0	
Urea	46·7				

BIBLIOGRAPHY
BOOKS

GENERAL

Commercial Hydroponics, by M. Bentley (Johannesburg).

Complete Book of the Greenhouse, by Ian G. Walls.

Growing Plants in Nutrient Solutions, by W. I. Turner and V. A. Henry (New York, 1939).

Growing Plants Without Soil, by M. Bentley (Johannesburg).

Hydroponics—the Bengal System, by J. Sholto Douglas.

Profitable Growing Without Soil, by H. F. Hollis.

Soilless Culture, by T. Saunby (1953).

Soilless Gardening for Flat and Home, by M. Bentley (Johannesburg, 1957).

Soilless Growth of Plants, by C. Ellis and M. W. Swaney, 2nd ed (New York, 1953).

Successful Gardening Without Soil, by C. E. Ticquet (1952).

The Complete Guide to Soilless Gardening, by W. F. Gericke (New York, 1940).

SPECIFIC

Hunger Signs in Crops, G. Hambridge, editor (Washington, DC).

pH and Plants, by J. Small (1946).

Sand and Water Culture Methods used in the Study of Plant Nutrition, by E. J. Hewitt, 2nd ed (1965).

The Diagnosis of Mineral Deficiencies in Plants by Visual Symptoms, by T. Wallace (1951).

CIRCULARS AND BULLETINS

'Automatically Operated Sand Culture Equipment', by F. M.

Eaton, Dept of Agric Publication G—1023 (Washington).

'Gravel Crops', by V. Ball (West Chicago, 1939).

'Gravel Crops and Sub-irrigation', by V. Ball (West Chicago, 1941).

'Growing Ornamental Greenhouse Crops in Gravel Culture', by D. C. Kiplinger and A. Laurie, Ohio Agric Expt Sta Bul 634 (Wooster, Ohio, 1942).

'Growing Plants in Nutrient Solution', by L. J. Alexander, V. H. Morris and H. C. Young, Spec Circ 56, Ohio Agric Expt Sta (Wooster, Ohio, 1939).

'Hydroponic Culture of Vegetable Crops', by J. G. Stout and M. E. Marvel, Circ 192, Agric Exten Service (Gainesville, Florida, 1959).

'Hydroponics: The Science of Growing Crops without Soil', by J. P. Biebel, Bull 180, Dept of Agric (Tallahassee, 1960).

'If They Could Speak'. Chilean Nitrate Educational Bureau Inc (New York).

'Methods of Growing Plants in Solution and Sand Cultures', by J. W. Shive and W. R. Robbins, Bull 636, New Jersey Agric Expt Sta, Rutgers University (New Brunswick, NJ, 1948).

'Nutriculture', by R. B. and A. P. Withrow, Circ 328, Purdue University Agric Expt Sta (Lafayette, Indiana, 1948).

'Nutrient Solution Methods of Greenhouse Crop Production', by R. B. Withrow and J. P. Biebel, Circ 232, Purdue University Agric Expt Sta (Lafayette, Indiana, 1937).

'The Greenhouse Cultivation of Carnations in Sand', by H. M. Bickart and C. H. Connors, Bull 588, New Jersey Expt Sta (1935).

'The Water Culture Method of Growing Plants Without Soil', by D. R. Hoagland and D. I. Arnon, Circ 347, College of Agric, University of California (Berkeley, 1950).

SCIENTIFIC PAPERS

'A Sub-irrigation Method of Supplying Nutrient Solutions to Plants growing under Commercial and Experimental Conditions', by R. B. Withrow and J. P. Biebel, *J Agric Res*

(1936), **53**, 693.

'A Universal Method for Preparing Nutrient Solutions of a desired composition', by A. A. Steiner, *Plant and Soil* (1961), **15**, 134–54.

'Composition of the Tomato Plant as influenced by Nutrient Supply in relation to Fruiting', by D. I. Arnon and D. R. Hoagland, *Bot Gaz* (1943), **104**, 577.

'Crop Production in Artificial Culture Solutions and in Soils with special reference to factors influencing Yields and Absorption of Inorganic Nutrients', by D. I. Arnon and D. R. Hoagland, *Soil Sci* (1940), **50**, 463.

'Effect of Mineral Nutrition on the Ascorbic Acid Content of the Tomato', by K. C. Hamner, C. B. Lyon and C. L. Hamner, *Bot Gaz* (1942), **103**, 586.

'Large Scale Soilless Culture for Plant Research', by O. W. Davidson, *Soil Sci* (1946), **62**, 71.

'Nutrient Culture of Crop Plants', by R. H. Stoughton, *Agriculture* (1947), **53**, 539.

'Plant Growth with Nutrient Solution: I. Comparison of Pure Sand and Fresh Soil as the Aggregate for Plant Growth', by R. M. Woodman and D. A. Johnson, *J Agric Sci* (1946), **36**, 80.

'The Culture of Plants in Sand and in Aggregate', by R. O. Miles, *Bull Jealots Hill Res Sta*, **2** (Rev) (1947).

'The Effect of Root Aeration on Plant Growth', by R. E. Williamson, *Soil Sci Proc* (1964), **28**, 86–90

'The Nutrient Value of Plants Grown With and Without Soil', by D. I. Arnon, H. D. Simms and A. F. Morgan, *Soil Sci* (1947), **63**, 129.

'The Use of Brackish Water in Hydroponic Systems', by M. Schwarz, *Plant and Soil* (1963), **19**, 166–73.

INDEX

indicator paper, 111
indicator solutions, 111
preference, 109-10
recommended, 109
scale, 109
what is, 108
Phosphate treatment of gravel, 177
Phosphorus, 21, 22, 130
Photoperiod, 123, 196
Photosynthesis, 17
Plant food (*see also* Nutrient
solution), 54, 90-1
commercial, 33, 140
making the, 54-6
mixing, 92
rate of use, 92
Plant growth chamber, 203
Plants
acid types, 109
cells, 11-12
light requirements, 63
make-up of, 11 et seq
Plasmolysis, 14
Plastic pots, 50
Polythene bags, 172-3
Potassium, 21, 22, 130
Potassium/nitrogen ratio, 130
Pot plants, 156-9
Protoplasm, 11, 12
Pump, 82, 86
Pumping
control of, 90
PVC fittings, 82

R

Rainfall, 63, 122
Relative humidity, 199
wet-and-dry bulb thermometer,
200, 201, 202
Reservoir
capacity, 87
height below tank, 84
water adjustment, 90
water loss, 90
working level of, 92
Respiration, 19
Roots, 13-14, 16
removal of residues, 99

Rose, 154-6
disbudding, 155
pests, 155-6
planting, 154
pruning, 155
types, 154
Running costs, 93

S

Sachs, 26
Salts
forms of, 127-8
Sand, 45
lime test for, 45
treatment of, 45
Sand culture, 37
Sealing of joints, 98
Sea-water
composition of, 106
Seed germination, 70-71
Seedlings
damping off, 74
feeding, 74
in vermiculite, 71-6
sowing in gravel, 94
thinning out, 75
transplanting, 52, 75
Seed trays
plastic, 72
preparation of, 71-2
types, 72
Site
choice of, 78, 123
Soil
humus in, 15
inorganic part, 15
make-up, 16
organic part, 15
Spraying, 178-9
Sprays
compatability of, 179
emulsion, 178
mixing, 124
wettable powders, 178
Staking, 64, 121
Stamens, 20
Stem, 16-17